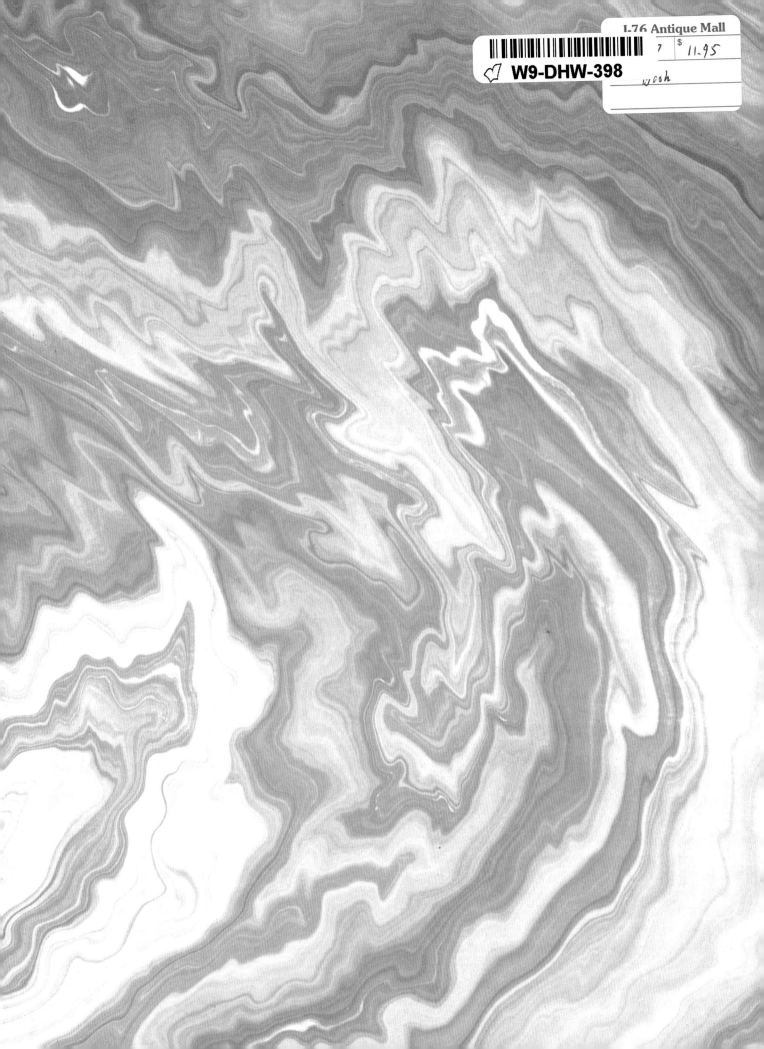

Antique Linens

From the Kitchen to the Boudoir

Marsha L.
Manchester

Schiffer
Publishing Ltd

4880 Lower Valley Road, Atglen, PA 19310 USA

Dedication

To my father who I only knew for sixteen years, Primo Guillio Viola. To my grandmother who I still enjoy at ninety-nine years, Fannie Canelli Viola.

Designed by "Sue"
Type set in Bernard Mod BT/Souvenir Lt BT

ISBN: 0-7643-1691-5
Printed in China
1 2 3 4

Published by Schiffer Publishing Ltd.
4880 Lower Valley Road
Atglen, PA 19310
Phone: (610) 593-1777; Fax: (610) 593-2002
E-mail: Schifferbk@aol.com
Please visit our web site catalog at
www.schifferbooks.com
We are always looking for people to write books on new and related subjects. If you have an idea for a book, please contact us at the above address.

This book may be purchased from the publisher.
Include $3.95 for shipping.
Please try your bookstore first.
You may write for a free catalog.

In Europe, Schiffer books are distributed by
Bushwood Books
6 Marksbury Avenue
Kew Gardens
Surrey TW9 4JF England
Phone: 44 (0) 20 8392 8585
Fax: 44 (0) 20 8392 9876
E-mail: Bushwd@aol.com
Free postage in the UK. Europe: air mail at cost.

Contents

Acknowledgments

To Estelle Goldman, a lovely lady who also loves linens. To Susan Crago for helping me at the very last minute. To Tracy Jesus for lending me special items from her personal collection. To Maura Metz who shared a wonderful early textile to be photographed. To Maria Arata for her generous loan. To Graham Gavert for his passion of fine linens. To Ellen Raiselis who also has a passion for vintage linens. To Susan Curran-Wright who has been my friend for many years. To Annette Bithoney who trusted me with her linens. To Janice Liljestrand for sharing her knowledge with me. To Verna Scott for her expertise and generosity. To Linda Stevenson, a great neighbor and an excellent photographer. And finally, to Byron E. Bruffee for his patience and love. Thank you all.

Introduction

From the moment we wake up on crisp, line dried linen sheets with delicate lace edging, to drying ourselves with thick, plush, terrycloth cotton towels, to dressing ourselves for the day in silk, we surround ourselves with fabrics. They fill our lives and our homes with comfort and beauty. From the moment the flax is spun and the cotton bolls are woven, a glorious fabric is in the making for a sumptuous linen bath towel or a stately banquet dining cloth with twenty-four matching napkins. So versatile is linen that we use it for our finest dining table, our most humble daily kitchen cloths, and the sheets that engulf us before we nod off to sleep at night. Indeed, linens embrace our lives.

When I started collecting vintage linens over three decades ago there were no price guides available. Looking back now, I realize the many, albeit valuable mistakes I made. With this broad-based price guide there will be no more guessing or costly errors. You will have the knowledge and confidence to purchase that beautiful pillowcase set or those lovely Battenberg Lace net curtains. Before you know it, the inescapable richness and luxury of fine linens will adorn your life and the more you have, the more you will want.

The linens in this book were gathered and photographed to encourage an awareness and appreciation of their use. I have assembled a collection of lacy confections to time honored yet practical linens meant for everyday use. These are not museum quality pieces. They are well-loved, well-used items spun from the nimble fingers of a five-year-old apprentice to the deft skilled hands of an accomplished needlewoman. I have also included a few items from unskilled factory workers. The timeless beauty of these cherished items shows in the gloss of the timeworn fabrics. All items represented are in perfect condition. Since vintage linens can either be factory made by the dozens or be one-of-a-kind items, I have given a range of sizes, colors, and embellishments in the photo captions. The smaller, less fancy items would fit into the lower price range.

Dating linens is very difficult unless they come with their original tags or receipt of purchase. When acquiring items, I would ask the previous owner of their recollection of the age, use, location of purchase, and any pertinent information about them. Through dealers and collectors willing to share their expertise, knowledge, and linens, I was able to compile to the best of my ability accurate descriptions, dates, and prices. With estate sales, on-line auctions, and live auctions, there seems to be an even greater desire to collect only the best available. My advice is to buy it if you love it. Often age doesn't matter with vintage linens. As long as the fibers are strong, sturdy, and without damage, go ahead, use it and enjoy it, you will be glad that you did.

The Linens

ANTIMACASSAR - A three-piece set used on upholstered chairs to protect the two arms from hand soil and the back from the heavy oil men used on their hair. It is easier to wash these pieces than to constantly wash the upholstery. These pieces can also be used on a vanity, dresser, or as a sideboard set.

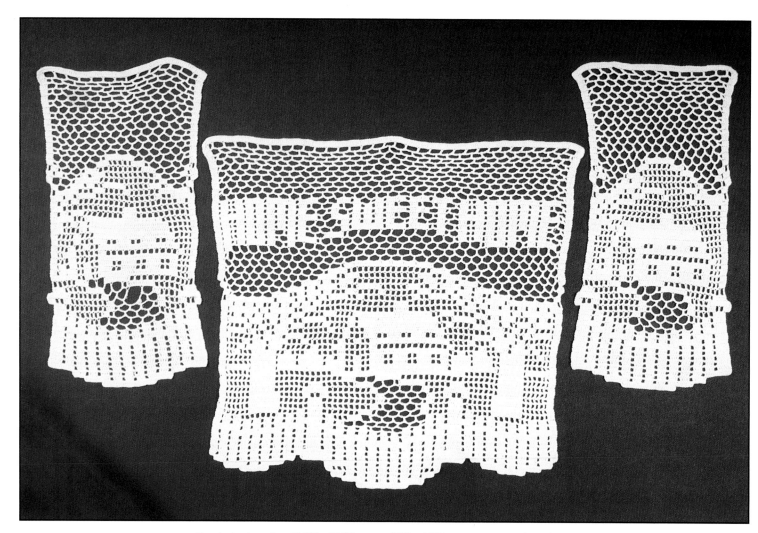

Crochet - America, 12"W x 10"D, arms 6"W x 10"D, cream cotton thread with verse "HOME SWEET HOME" from a pattern book, c. 1915-1950, $25-35.

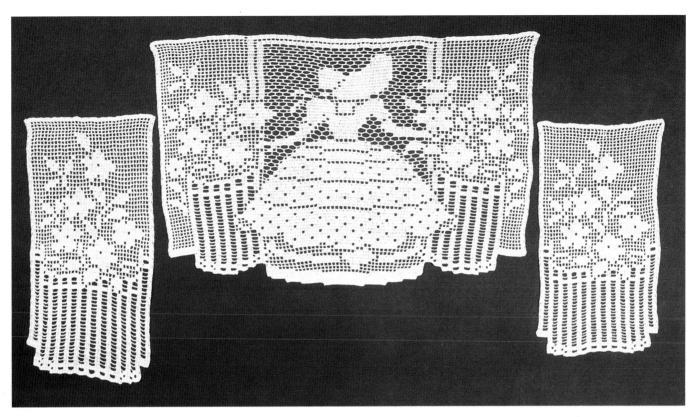

Crochet - America, 16"W x 9"D, arms 5"W x 9"D, figural Southern Belle with a bonnet in a garden on soft cream linen with cotton crochet thread from a pattern book, c. 1915-1950, $25-35.

Lace - Italy/Belgium, 16"W x 12"D, white cotton thread in Italian or Belgium Zele needle lace, c. 1900-1940, $35-40.

Linen - China, 18"W x 12"D, linen fabric cross stitched with embroidery
floss in multiple colors with arm pieces, c. 1925-1960, $15-25.

Linen - Italy/China, 16"W x 11"D,
arms 7"W x 11"D, factory made
on white linen fabric with
cutwork, embroidery, needle lace,
and lace edge, c. 1915-1950,
$35-45; with arm pieces, $45-55.

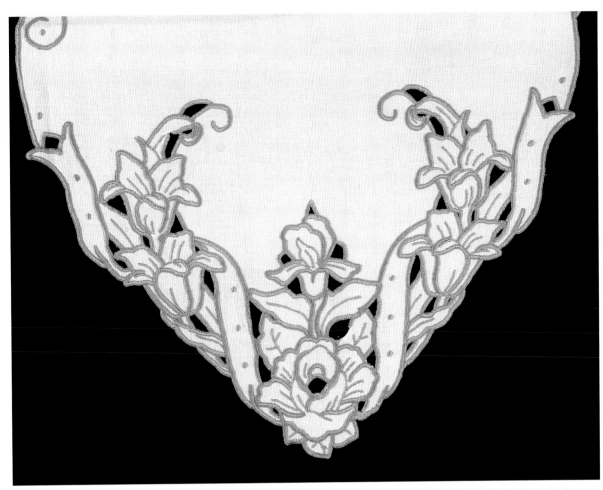

Linen - Portugal, 16"W x 14"D, hand-made cutwork and embroidery on ecru linen with taupe cotton embroidery floss and matching arm pieces, c. 1915-1955, $30-45.

Machine Made - America, 16"W x 14"D, white or cream cotton thread, c. 1910-1945, $15-20; with arm pieces, $25-35.

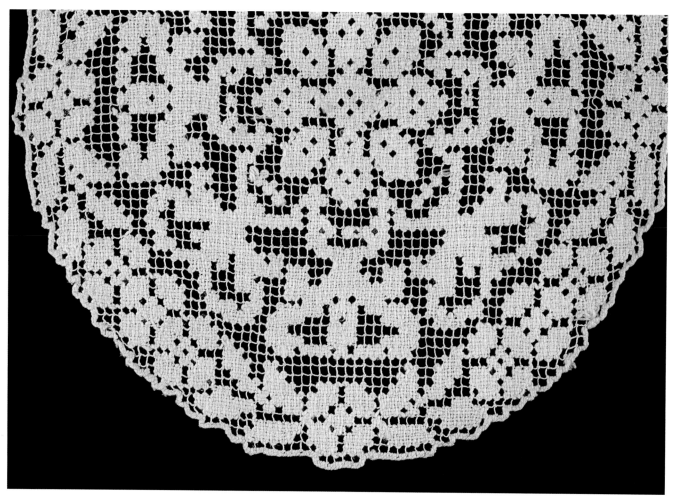

Net Darning - China, 17"W x 13"D, white or ivory cotton thread hand woven on a machine net background with matching arm pieces, c. 1930-1960, $20-30.

Also available:

Alençon - France, 16"W x 12"D, machine made lace with a delicate cream net mesh ground, hand run needle lace design, outlined with cordonnets, and matching arm pieces, c. 1890-1985, $55-85.

Normandy - France, 15"W x 12"D, hand assembled multiple patchwork lace in cream cotton with matching arm pieces, c. 1915-1950, $75-95.

Tape Lace - Belgium, 16"W x 12"D, white cotton pre-made tapes with spider web fillings and matching arm pieces, c. 1925-1945, $45-60.

Quaker Lace - America, 16"W x 14"D, machine shuttled white or ivory cotton thread, c. 1932-1960, $10-20; with matching arm pieces, set $15-25.

BABY'S SWADDLING TIE - Used to bind a baby's navel in place, thus the ties are on one end only.

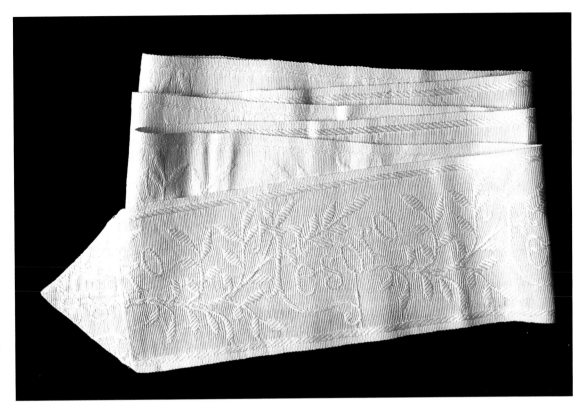

Cotton - Italy, 72"L x 6"W, "TESORO" or "AMORE" woven into the fabric, c. 1880-1950, $20-30. *Courtesy of Estelle Goldman and Susan Crago.*

BED COVERS - Other names are bedspreads, coverlets, duvets, Marseilles, Matlassés, and counterpanes. Today's use is more decorative than functional. Their first purpose was to protect the feather down comforter or wool blanket from dust and soil. The demand today is for the fanciest, the prettiest, and the most decorative.

Chenille - America, double size 104"L x 94"W, solid color or two tone in short fiber pile cotton, c. 1935-1965, $50-100; twin size 98"L x 82"W, $35-65. *Collection of Tracy Jesus.*

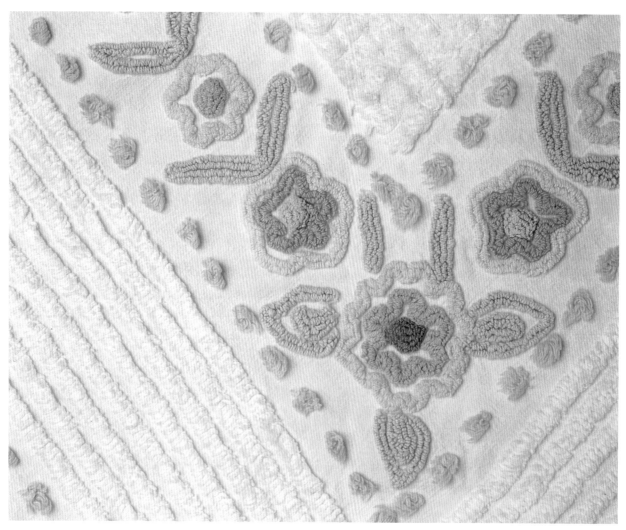

Chenille - America, twin size 104"L x 76"W, floral pattern in multiple colors on cotton, c. 1940-1970, $75-100; a pair $150-200. *Collection of Tracy Jesus.*

Chenille Baby Crib Cover - America, 66"L x 42"W, pastel color with a bunny, dog, kitty, or any children's motif, c. 1940-1960, $40-75. *Courtesy of Judith Greason.*

Coverlet - America, 95"L x 90"W, cotton four post cutout corners always with a matching layover pillow sham in a machine woven flat floral or geometric design with a scalloped edge, c. 1910-1950, $125-175.

Coverlet - America, double size 88"L x 84"W, machine made Trapunto-type with a raised floral or geometric design in white cotton, c. 1880-1950, $150-250; queen size 100"L x 90"W, $250-350.

Coverlet - America, queen or king size 106"L x 98"W (rare), extra large
machine made Trapunto-style white cotton coverlet with an inside woven area
of colored cotton in a floral or geometric pattern, c. 1880-1950, $400-500.

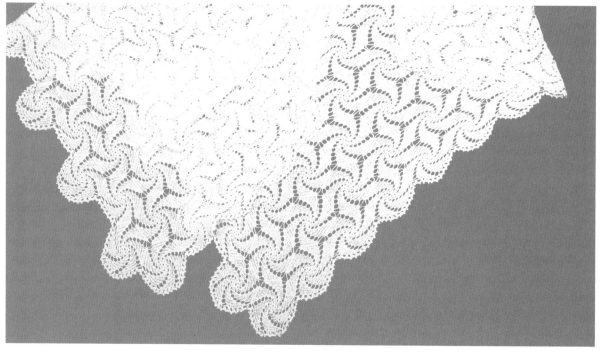

Crochet - America, double size 110"L x 90"W, popcorn, swirl, or Irish Rose pattern in
white or ecru cotton crochet, all accomplished by the dexterous fingers of needleworkers,
c. 1900-1960, $175-275; twin size 110"L x 80"W, $100-200; pair of twin size $175-275.

Embroidery - America, double size 110"L x 90"W, made from a kit with colored embroidery floss on cream cotton muslin, any pattern, c. 1915-1945, $75-150; twin size 110"L x 75"W, $50-75; pair of twin size $75-125.

Beautiful thickly padded stitches on natural cream linen, Great Britain, 110"L x 98"W, c. 1880, $150-350.

Net Darning - Italy, queen or double size 116"L x 110"W, ecru cotton needle run thread with a hand woven design on a machine net mesh background of frolicking cherubs, figures, or a floral pattern, c. 1900-1940, $250-350.

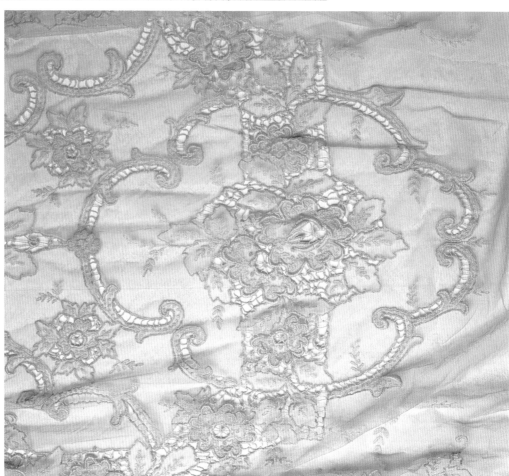

Net Lace - Germany/Belgium/France, 104"L x 88"W, cream network with tambour stitching, cutwork, embroidery, and/or cotton appliqués, c. 1910-1940, double size $250-350; pair of twins $300-400.

Normandy Lace - France, double size 104"L x 84"-98"W, multiple patchwork strips of white or ivory machine made Paris Lace creatively arranged with embroidered centerpieces of the Normandy region ladies' caps they wore on their heads, c. 1900-1945, $400-600; twin size $250-350; pair of twins $550-750.

Normandy Lace - France, 98"L x 88"W, sweet simplicity of white or ivory machine made Paris Lace with embroidered circles of the Normandy region lace, c. 1900-1945, twin, $75-150; double, $150-250.

Organdy - Switzerland, 108"L x 90"W, gossamer white cotton organdy with tucks, ruffles, and matching pillow shams with button closures, c. 1910-1950, $200-300.

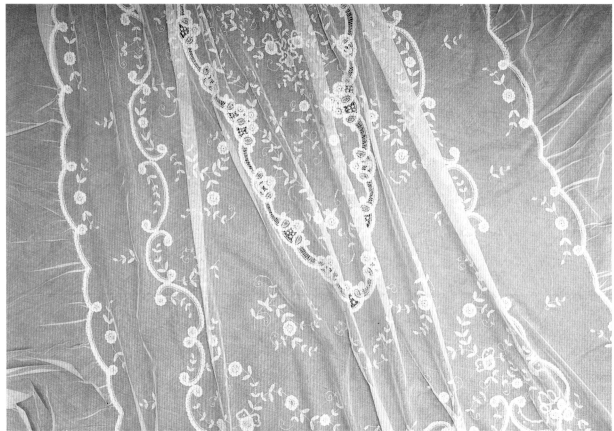

Princesse Lace - France/Belgium, 102"L x 98"W, machine made net mesh background in cream or white with hand appliquéd premade tapes of rosettes, scrollwork, and leaflet sprigs imitating Duchesse Lace, c. 1900-1950, double size $300-400; pair of twins $350-450.

Satin - France, 98"L x 88"W, twin size pastel silk or rayon fabric with strips of machine made Alençon lace, often with appliquéd monograms, c. 1915-1945, $60-80; pair, $75-100.

Seersucker - America, puckered cotton bed covers for summer cottage and camp use, c. 1920-1950, double size $25-35; pair of twins, $30-40.

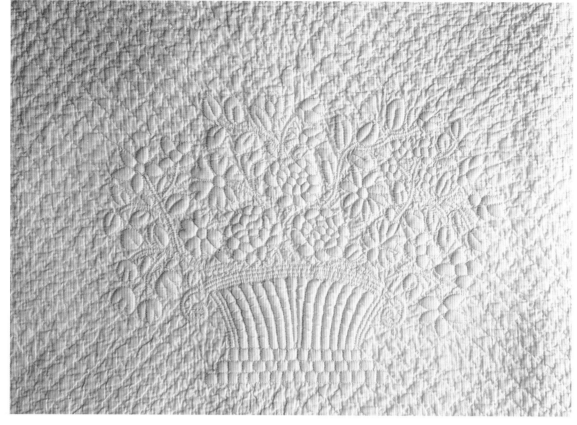

Trapunto - Italy, 88"L x 88"W, double layer fine percale white cotton of highly raised early patterns with cotton batting hand stuffed from the backside, c. 1825-1895, $1,000-1,500. *Courtesy of Maura Metz.*

Also available:

Candlewick - New England, double size 106"L x 86"W, handmade cotton French knots on off-white muslin, c. 1840-1900, $200-400; pair of matching twins 100"L x 68"W, $400-500.

Chenille - America, double or queen size 106"L x 96"W, pink rose buds with multiple green leaves on white cotton, c. 1940-1960, $150-200; twin size 98"L x 76"W, $100-150.

Chenille - America, double size 104"L x 94"W, double peacocks in multiple vibrant colors on cotton, c. 1940-1960, $150-250.

Chenille - America, double size 104"L x 94"W, satin background with cotton chenille floral design in any color, c. 1935-1965, $85-135; pair of twin size 100"L x 78"W, $100-200.

Counterpane - America, 90"L x 80"W, hand quilting on white cotton muslin with no inside batting, c. 1850-1910, $200-400.

Coverlet - America, queen or double size 100"L x 90"W, machine woven floral or geometric pattern in white cotton, c. 1880-1950, $100-200.

Coverlet - America, twin size 90"L x 75"W, white cotton with a machine woven floral pattern, c. 1920-1960, $75-125; pair $200-300.

Coverlet - America, double size 90"L x 80"W, white cotton with a machine stamped waffle weave, c. 1920-1950, $50-75; twin size 90"L x 68"W, $35-55.

Knit Lace - America, double or queen size 115"L x 98"W, intricate lacy confections fabricated with white or ivory cotton thread, c. 1920-1950, $200-300.

Linen - United Kingdom, queen or double size 110"L x 100"W, hand or machine embroidery, rows of drawnwork, and frothy filet crochet inserts on white linen, c. 1900-1950, $250-350.

Marseilles - France, 100"L x 80"-90"W, fine muslin cotton with machine stamped and raised floral patterns in a dash and dot design, c. 1850-1900, $250-450.

Needle Lace - Italy/France, 120"L x 90"-110"W, soft white cotton thread with cherub and/or female figures frolicking and playing instruments, c. 1900-1940, $400-600.

BIRD CAGE COVER - Having domestic birds in the home was quite common and pleasurable. To keep the birds warm at night, special covers were made to snugly fit their cage. They were usually purchased through a ladies magazine. These home assembly packages came complete with directions, stamped embroidery designs, muslin fabric, cotton embroidery floss, and piping.

Embroidered - America, colorful embroidery on muslin, c. 1900-1965, $25-45.

BISCUIT KEEPERS - These unusually shaped pieces were placed on the bottom of a bread basket, the hot biscuits were placed inside the linen keepers, and the four sides were brought up and around the biscuits to keep them warm yet letting the steam rise.

Scone Keeper - United Kingdom, about 12" round, eyelet cotton with multiple pie-shaped pockets to keep the scones warm, c. 1920-present, $15-25.

Also available:

Linen - Portugal, about 18"L x 18"W, hand embroidered "HOT BISCUITS" on linen, c. 1915-1975, $10-25.

BLANKET COVERS - These practical yet decorative items were meant to protect precious wool blankets from wear, tear, dust, and soil. It is always easier to wash a blanket cover rather than a wool blanket.

Cotton - America, 81"L x 72"W, two pieces of printed cotton sewn shut on three sides with the fourth side having snaps to enclose the blanket or comforter, c. 1920-1970, $55-75.

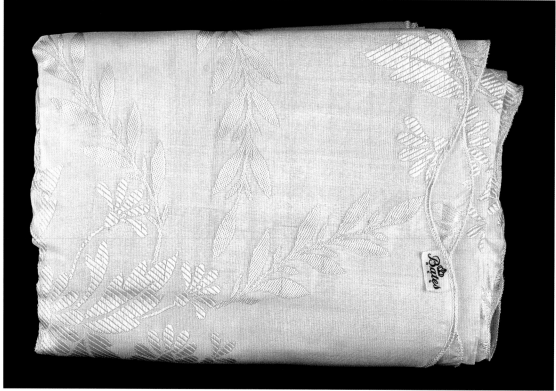

Satin - America, double size 90"L x 80"W, made by the Bates Company in pastel colors with an inexpensive lace border or a scalloped edge, c. 1920-1950, $15-25.

Satin - France, 88"L x 82"W, pastel colors with insertions of French Alençon
lace, c. 1900-1945, $50-70; pair of twins, 88"L x 68"W, $65-85.

Also available:

Cotton - America, double size 90"L x 80"W, two pieces of cotton sewn together on all four sides with a center opening about 12"-18" surrounded by fancy embroidery, c. 1880-1940, $35-45; pair of twins 90"L x 68"W, $45-55.

BOLSTER CASE - An extra long tube case that could be cut in half to make two pillowcases. Small bolster boudoir cases can also be cylindrical. Old bolster cases now fit our modern body pillows.

Boudoir - Europe, 16"L x 12"W, cylindrical in shape with ruffles, cutwork, embroidery, and lace insertions with a button closure on the finest linen available, c. 1880-1940, $55-85.

Cotton - America, 64"L x 22"W, muslin, with or without lace or monograms, c. 1890-1955, $20-30.

Linen - Ireland, 78"L x 24"W, fine linen with embroidery, lace, and/or monograms on both ends, c. 1900-1950, $75-95.

Tube - England, 70"L x 21"W, seamless linen/cotton blend with floral handmade or machine stitched embroidery on both ends, c. 1900-1950, $75-95.

BOOK COVER - Fabric covers made to protect special books.

Linen - America, 12"H x 6"W, hand painted flowers on linen fabric, c.1870-1940, $25-45.

Linen - Ireland, 15"H x 7"W, floral printed linen fabric, c. 1870-1945, $25-45.

BOUDOIR CASES - Delicate bedroom adornments that come in all shapes, sizes, and fabrics lavishly decorated with lace, cutwork, embroidery, and ruffles.

Machine Made Lace - America, 14"-18" round, rectangular, or heart shaped with cherubs pulling chariots or playing musical instruments on ivory cotton lace with original satin pillow, c. 1890-1940, $75-95.

Net Lace - Belgium/ France/Germany, 16"-20"L x 12"-16"W, ivory mesh net background with tambour stitched cotton appliqués and cutwork, also know as Novelty Lace, c. 1900-1945, $55-75; round, $60-80.

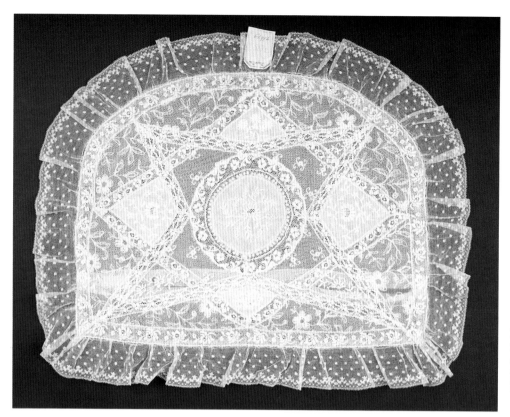

Normandy Lace - France, 16"-20"W x 12"-16"L, half moon, rectangular, or round shape with hand assembled patchwork of white or cream frothy Paris Lace, c. 1880-1955, $75-125.

Roaring Twenties - America, 18" round, rectangular, or heart shaped with pastel shading on cotton, lace, and colored hand embroidery often with a woman's image, c. 1905-1945, $35-45.

Also available:

Heart Shape - France, 16"W x 10"D, sheer white linen with two appliquéd hearts, monogram, cutwork, and embroidery with a lace edge, c. 1900-1950, $65-85.

BREAD TRAY MATS - These can be placed under the bread in a tray or placed on top to keep the heat in yet allowing the steam to escape.

Crocheted "BREAD" or "STAFF OF LIFE" - America, 10"-16"L x 4"-6"W, oval or rectangular white or cream cotton thread, c. 1920-1945, $15-20.

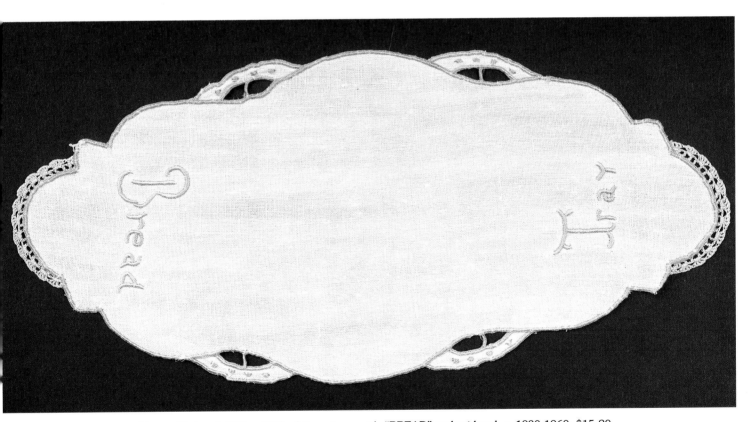

Linen - Portugal, 12"L x 6"W, white or ivory with "BREAD" embroidered, c. 1930-1960, $15-20.

Linen - America, 12"L x 8"W, hand cross stitched "BREAD" on cream linen, c. 1915-1955, $10-15.

BRIDGE SETS - As the parlor game of Bridge became popular in the 1920s, there was a need for fancy card table covers 32"-48" square with matching napkins. We now use these sets as table toppers.

Damask - Czechoslovakia, 48"L x 48"W, linen damask with drawn threads, six napkins, and six coasters, c. 1930-1970, $65-85. *Collection of Ellen Raiselis.*

Linen - Italy, 28"-42" square, four to six matching napkins on white linen with cutwork, embroidery, and a needle lace center, c. 1920-1970, $45-65.

Linen - Italy, 28"-48" square, beige linen with taupe, olive, gray, or dark brown embroidery, c. 1920-1970, $20-30.

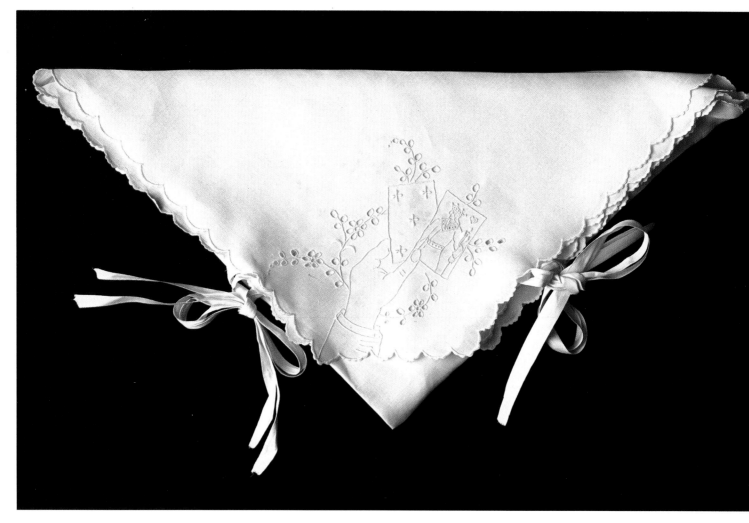

Linen - Portugal, 42"L x 42"W, white Irish linen with white embroidery of a hand holding a deck of cards with ties for the four corners to secure the cloth to the table, c. 1920-1960, $50-75. *Courtesy of Annette Bithoney.*

Opposite page:
Organdy - Portugal, 36"L x 36"W, cotton organdy with pastel appliqués, embroidery, and matching napkins, never used, c. 1930-1970, $50-100.

Also available:

Cotton - America, 28"-48" square, four to six matching napkins, white or ivory fabric with hand embroidery and/or appliqués made from a store bought kit, c. 1915-1945, $20-30.

Linen - China, 28"-48" square, Oriental motif cross-stitched with bright cotton embroidery floss, c. 1920-1955, $10-20.

Linen - Portugal, 28"-48" square, white or cream linen with white, blue, or taupe embroidery with a basket, floral urn, or butterfly pattern often with ties at the corner for securing the cloth to the table legs, c. 1920-1960, $40-60.

BUREAU SCARF - Mostly rectangular in shape, these were meant to protect the furniture's surface.

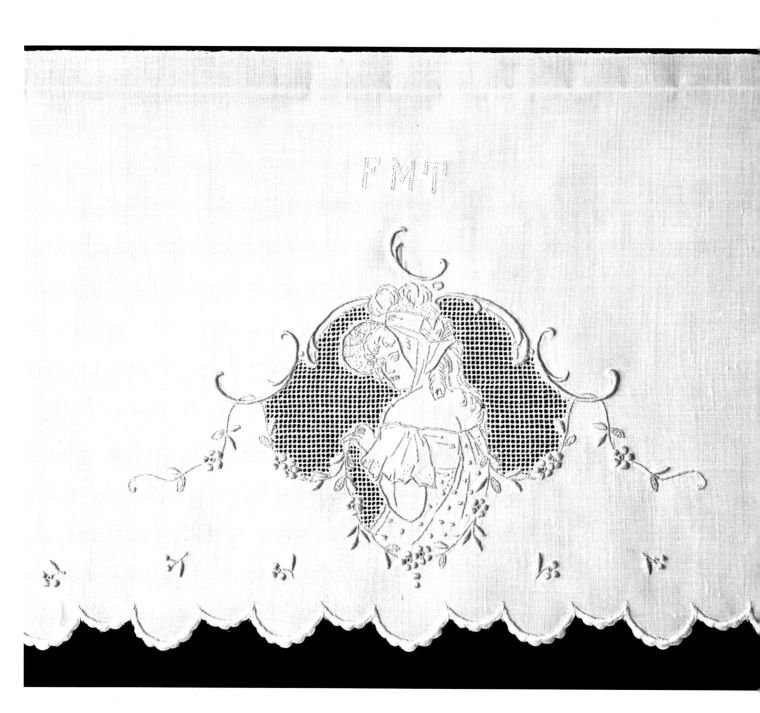

Opposite page and above:
Appenzell - Switzerland, 32"-60"L x 15"-17"W, quite possibly the world's finest elaborate embroidery on linen with Buratto lattice work and a monogram of FMT, c. 1900-1970, floral, $150-200; figural $200-300.

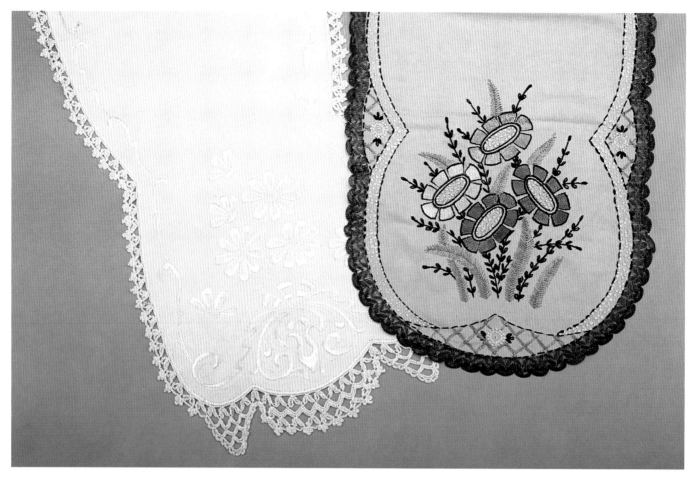

Arts & Crafts - United Kingdom, 34"-54"L x 16"-19"W, natural flax colored linen with colorful stylized hand embroidery, often with lace edges, c. 1890-1915, $75-150.

Chemical Lace - Germany, 32"-60"L x 16"W, machine made Plauen Lace with a chemically removed foundation with very lovely floral patterns made to imitate old world lace, c. 1870-1955, $30-45.

Crochet Lace - America, 28"-60"L x 12"-20"W, very fine filet handmade cream or white cotton lace in any lovely pattern with or without a linen center, c. 1915-present, $20-35.

Cutwork - Portugal, 54"L x 17"W, fine white Irish linen with hand embroidered bows, French knots, padded satin stitching, cutwork, and a monogram, c. 1900-1970, $55-75.

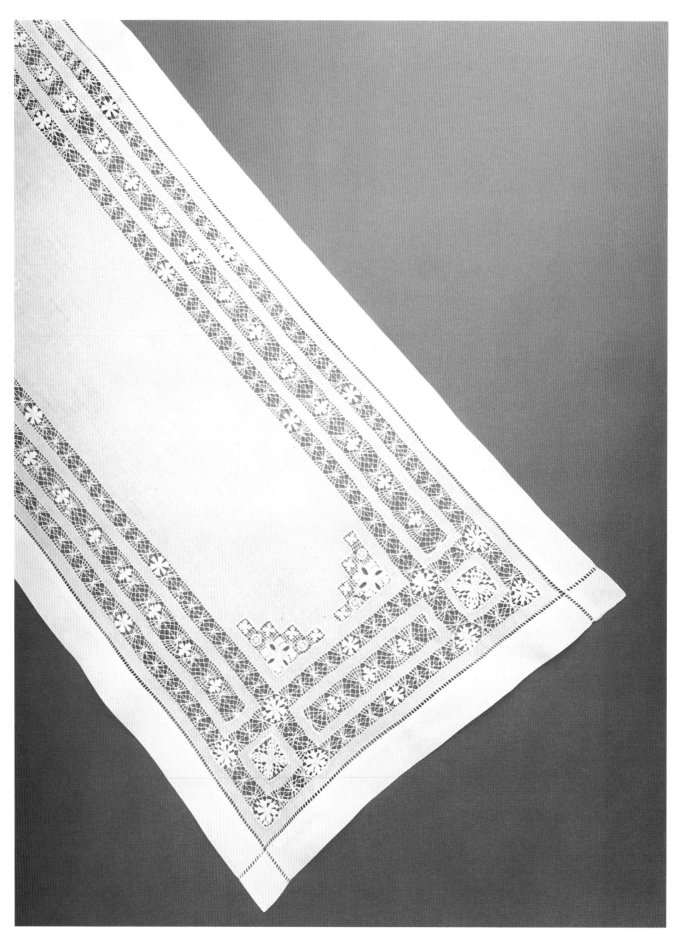

Drawnwork - Canary Islands, 28"-66"L x 15"-20"W, hand drawn threads
with Tenerife Lace corners mostly on white linen, c. 1890-1950, $35-55.

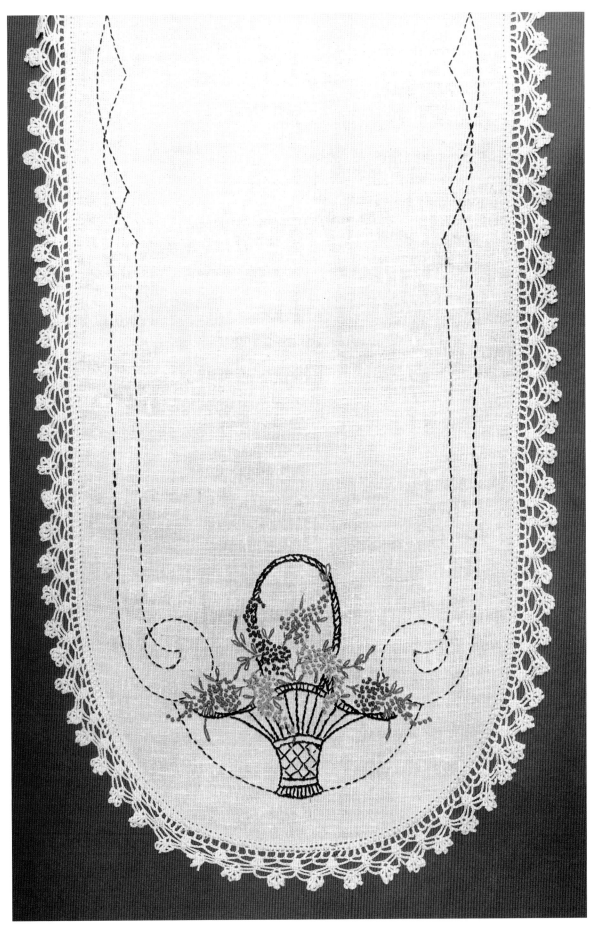

Embroidered - America, 28"-66"L x 14"-20"W, from a pre-stamped kit ordered from a ladies magazine, which has embroidered colored floss and added machine or handmade lace on fine cotton or linen, c. 1915-1955, $25-35.

Embroidered - America, 44"L x 18"W, Southern Belle pattern on cotton with colorful hand embroidery and a crochet lace insert panel for a skirt ordered from a ladies home magazine, c. 1915-1955, $25-55.

Embroidered - Portugal, 48"L x 18"W, fine Madeira hand embroidery with white, light blue, or beige cotton thread on white or ecru Irish linen in the basket, floral urn, or butterfly pattern, and often with a rose filet lace edge, c. 1900-1970, $25-75.

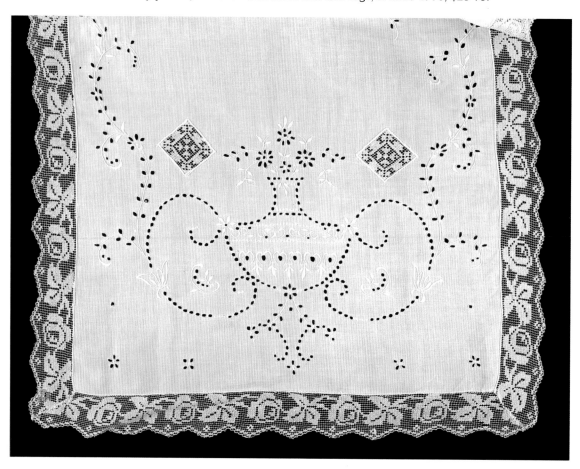

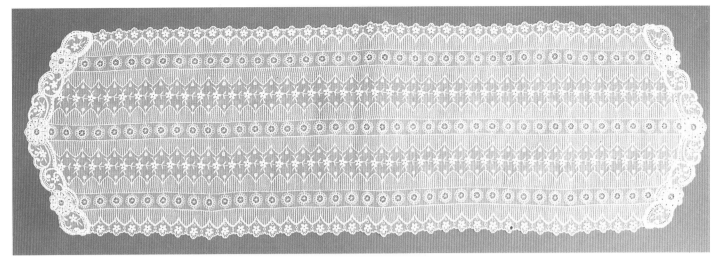

Eyelet Embroidery - America, 38"L x 14"W, machine stitching and cutwork
on white or cream nylon fabric, very practical, c. 1950-present, $15-25.

Filet Crochet Lace - United Kingdom, 28"-60"L x 12"-20"W, web spun floral
pattern hand crocheted with delicate cotton thread, c. 1900-1975, $25-45.

Machine Lace - America, 28"-54"L x 14"-18"W, drawnwork on white cotton fabric
with pretty but low quality machine made lace edge, c. 1930-1960, $10-20.

Machine Lace - America, 28"-48"L x 14"-18"W, raised flowers on ivory
mesh net background, very desirable, c. 1920-1960, $40-60.

Machine Lace - America, 28"-66"L x 14"-18"W, machine woven lace with beautiful patterns, often
with figures, on humble white cotton centers that are low quality, c. 1920-1955, $30-40.

Needle Lace - Italy/Belgium/France, 28"-66"L x 14"-18"W,
handmade figural white linen thread lace, c. 1900-1955, $65-85.

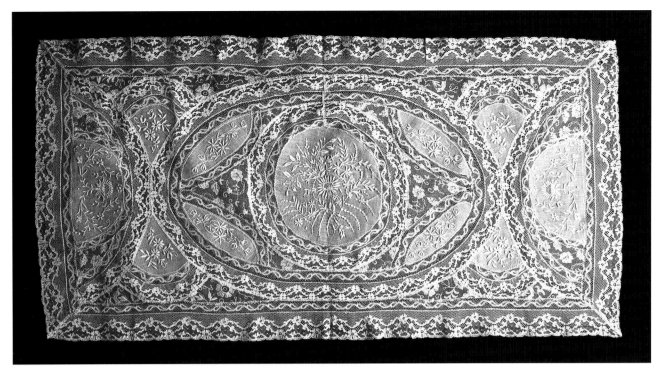

Normandy Lace - France, 32"-56"L x 14"-18"W, cream or white patchwork Paris Lace hand stitched together always with an embroidered fabric center depicting the regional caps that women wore, c. 1900-1950, $50-100.

Tape Lace - Belgium, 44"L x 16"W, pastel linen center, appliquéd Princess lace, tape lace border, and its label of origin, c. 1920-1950, $45-75.

Quaker Lace - America, 32"-66"L x 14"-18"W, machine shuttled cotton lacy patterns with picots on the edges that are made on Nottingham looms (invented in 1846 primarily for making lace curtains), c. 1930-1980, $15-25.

Also available:

Alençon - France, 36"L x 16"W, enchanting cream colored machine made needle lace with a delicate mesh ground, outlined with cordonnet cording, and linked with brides without picots, c. 1890-1985, $50-90.

Cutwork - France, 58"L x 18"W, fine Irish linen with hand embroidered bows, French knots, padded satin stitching, cutwork, and a monogram, c. 1900-1970, $50-90.

Mosaic - Italy, 28"-66"L x 14"-20"W, fine punchwork-type design with or without embroidery on linen, c. 1915-1965, $25-65.

Net Lace - America, 28"-66"L x 14"-18"W, machine woven mesh net background with tambour hand stitching, c. 1920-1965, $40-55.

Punchwork - China, 28"-66"L x 14"-18"W, a poor imitation of an Italian mosaic-type design on low quality cotton, c. 1930-1970, $10-15.

CARVING CLOTH - Rectangular cloths in patterned linen damask to be placed on the dinner table under the carving platter to catch any spills.

Linen - United Kingdom, 24"L x 16"W, fringed linen damask often with bands of color, c. 1860-1960, each $25-50.

COASTERS - Any shape or size doily to be used at the dinner table as a catch-all for spills from dinner plates, soup bowls, or stemware. These always came in sets of six, eight, and twelve.

Brussels Lace - Belgium/France, 6"-9" round, mesh net background with appliquéd Princess Lace with or without a fabric center, c. 1880-1950, each $10-12.

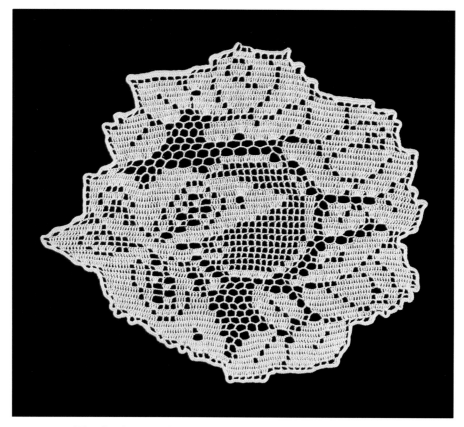

Filet Crochet - England, 6" round, fine filet work with roses and
a butterfly worked with cotton thread, c. 1900-1970, $8-10.

Linen - Ireland, 6"-9" round, white linen with white hand
or machine embroidery, c. 1900-1950, each $8-10.

Mixed Brussels Lace - Belgium/Flanders, 6"-9" round, white linen centers with mixed bobbin and needle lace, c. 1880-1960, each $10-12.

Normandy Lace - France, 6"-9" round, ivory or white multiple patchwork Paris Laces, c. 1900-1960, each $10-12.

Needle Lace - Italy/China, 6"-9" round, white or cream cotton lace, acorns usually woven into the Chinese pattern, c. 1900-1970, each $8-10.

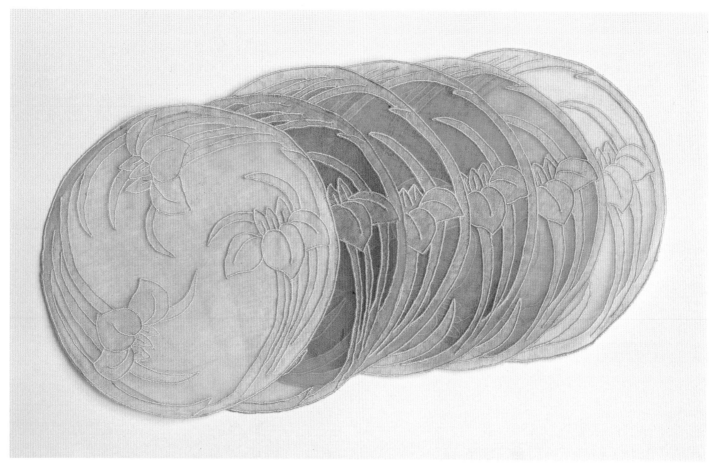

Organdy - Portugal, 6"-9" round, white, ivory, or soft pastel colors
with hand embroidery and appliqués, c. 1900-1960, each $8-10.

Rice Linen - China, 6"-9" round, white or cream rice linen (made from the
nettle plant) with cotton or silk hand embroidery, c. 1920-1960, each $5-7.

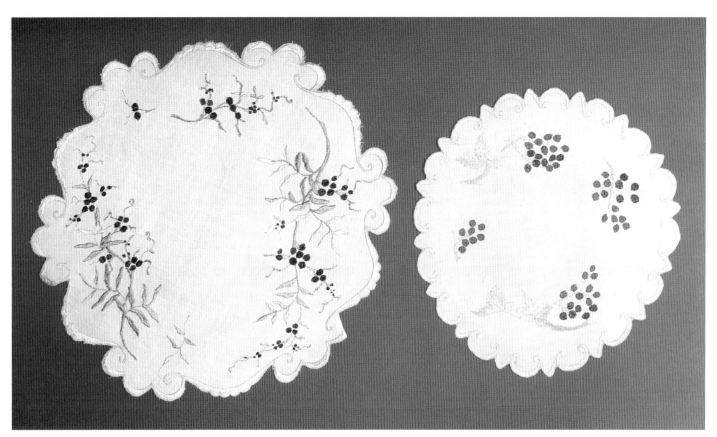

Society Silk Embroidery - America, 6"-9" round, beautiful silk floss hand embroidery on
fine Irish linen made only by skilled needlewomen of wealth, c. 1870-1925, each $10-12.

Tape Lace - Belgium, 6"-9" round, net lace center, tape lace edging,
and various spiderweb lace fillings, c. 1920-1950, each $8-10.

CORSET BAG - A custom made cover for ladies intimate apparel with a drawstring of satin ribbon.

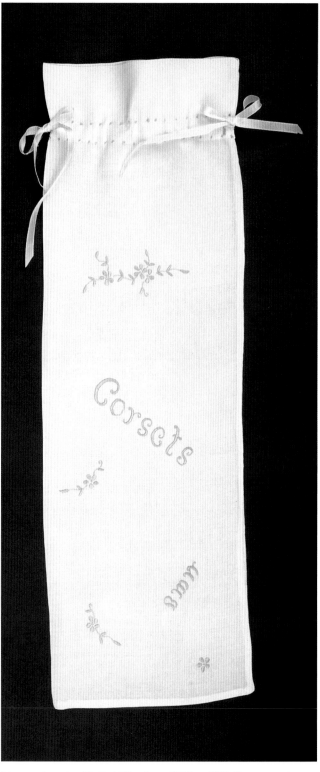

COMB-OUT COVER - European flaxen-fringed towels usually with colored bands, originally meant to be guest towels, that are custom cut for placement on the shoulders during hair brushing.

Fringed Towel - United Kingdom/Czechoslovakia, 22"L x 17"W, color bands often with hand embroidered combs and brushes with an added tie for the neck, c.1880-1920, $35-55.

Linen - America/United Kingdom, 26"L x 8"W, flowers and "CORSET" hand embroidered, c. 1875-1918, $75-85.

Also available:

Cotton - America, 24"L x 8"W, floral hand embroidery, c. 1880-1918, $40-60.

CRUMB COVERS - Silent butler covers to discreetly remove crumbs from the dining table.

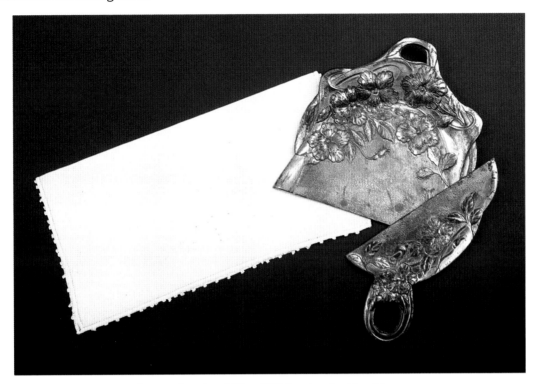

Linen - America, 10"L x 5"W, hand embroidered linen
cover to remove table crumbs, c. 1900-1950, $10-15.

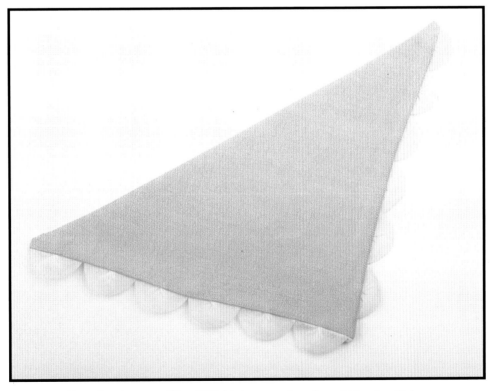

Triangle - America, 9"L x 5"W, fabric covered cardboard triangle with lace
only on two sides to scrape crumbs from the table, c.1900-1950, $10-15.

CURTAINS - To veil a room's interior, fabric was mounted to a window or door to provide privacy, soften the light, and let in air. The wealthier the household, the lacier the curtain.

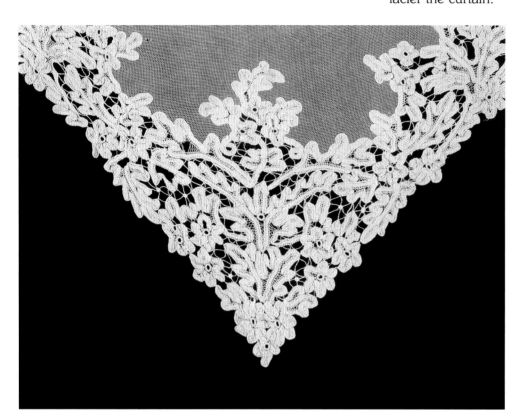

Lace - Belgium, 64"-110"L x 32"-48"W, cream mesh net lace background with hand appliquéd designs and tape lace, c. 1880-1950, one panel $90-125.

Lace - Belgium, 92"L x 38"W, white machine loomed mesh net lace background imitating hand cutwork, embroidery, and appliqués, c. 1880-1950, pair $200-300.

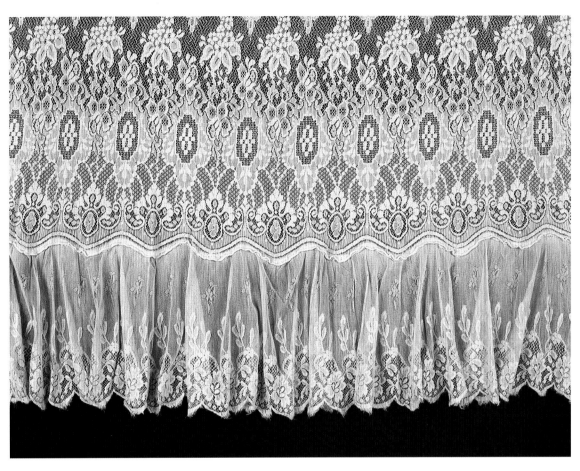

Lace - Nottingham, England, 64"-104"L x 30"-48"W, grand luxe white or cream colored machine made lace panels with floral or geometric patterns and a frothy lace flounce, c. 1880-1950, one panel $75-100.

Tambour - Switzerland, 64"-98"L x 32"-48"W, soft cambric cotton appliqués with machine made tambour backstitching, c. 1880-1970, one panel $75-125.

Valance - America, 48"L x 36"W, swag shaped Nottingham machine loomed floral pattern lace for a door or small window, c. 1930-1950, one panel, $45-65.

Also available:

Barkcloth - America, 74"-96"L x 32"-48"W, color printed nubby cotton cloth with bright beautiful flowers, c. 1930-1950, one panel $55-75.

Barkcloth - America, 74"-96"L x 32"-48"W, brightly printed nubby cotton cloth other than floral, c. 1930-1950, one panel $45-65.

Crochet - Europe, 24"-98"L to any width, hand crocheted white or cream cotton curtains from café to full window length, c. 1880-1970, one panel $25-100.

Dotted Swiss - America, 42"-90"L x 24"-48"W, cambric cotton resembling Switzerland's flocked dots, c. 1930-1960, one panel $10-20.

Hardanger - Norway, 48"-98"L x 32"-48"W, white counted thread drawnwork on white linen with satin stitches on kloster blocks, c. 1900-1960, one panel $50-75.

Lace - Eastern Europe, up to 120"L x up to 80"W, white or cream hand crocheted panel with net darning, drawnwork, and fringe for one large window, c. 1900-1960, $100-150.

DOILY - A decorative and utilitarian item named for a London textile merchant from the 1700s. They can be round, square, oblong, rectangle, or oval. Sizes vary from miniature up to 18" that can be any fabric or fiber.

Appenzell - Switzerland, 17" round, the finest whitework of figures and flowers with lattice Buratto work on supreme Irish linen, c. 1900-1970, $75-125.

Battenberg - Belgium, up to 18", cream or white linen center with cream or white pre-made tape lace, also called Modern Lace, c. 1860-1925, $25-45.

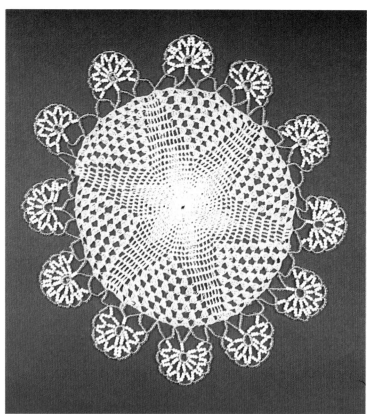

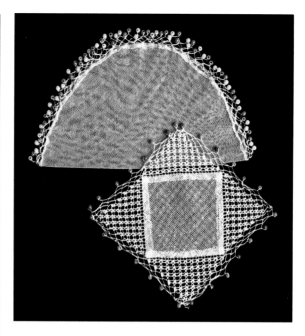

Left and above:
Beaded Edge - United Kingdom, 6"-12" round, cotton crochet or linen fabric with a row of weighted glass beads on the outside edge to place on top of pitchers and bowls to keep insects out, c. 1890-1980, $25-45.

Chemical Lace - Germany, up to 18", floral or figural cotton Plauen Lace with a chemically removed foundation made to imitate fancy old world lace, c. 1880-1950, $50-75.

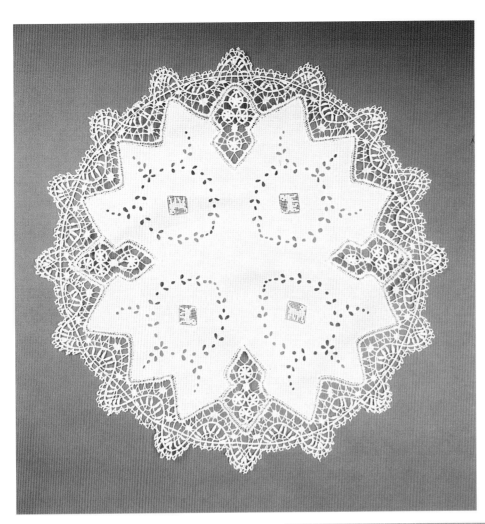

Cluny Lace - France, up to 18", bobbin made lace with geometric design rosettes, diamond blocks, and a braided loop edge with or without a linen center, c. 1860-1930, $25-35.

Coronation Cording - England, up to 18" round, white cotton machine made cording hand sewn inventively on a fabric background of linen, c. 1880-1925, $20-25.

Crochet - International, 17" star shaped, white cotton crochet thread, c. 1880-present, $20-30.

Crochet - England, 19"L x 16"W, fine filet crochet with animal figures, c. 1880-present, $15-25.

Crochet - America, 17" round, in any color or shape, c. 1900-present, $10-20.

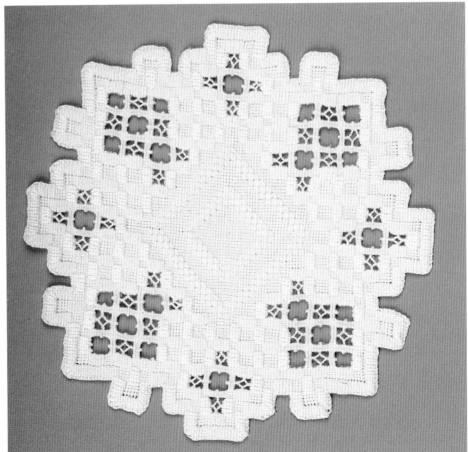

Hardanger - Norway, up to 18", white counted thread drawnwork on white linen with satin stitches on kloster blocks, c. 1900-1960, $20-30.

Knit Lace - America, up to 18" round, fine needles and fine cotton thread used for this difficult-to-make lace, c. 1880-1960, $20-30.

Machine Made Lace - America, up to 18", imitation of beautiful handmade old world lace without the cost of the original, c. 1870-1950, $25-35 .

Needle Lace - China, 14"L x 10"W, oval
needle lace doily in white or cream cotton
that is all hand assembled, c. 1920-1970,
$15-25.

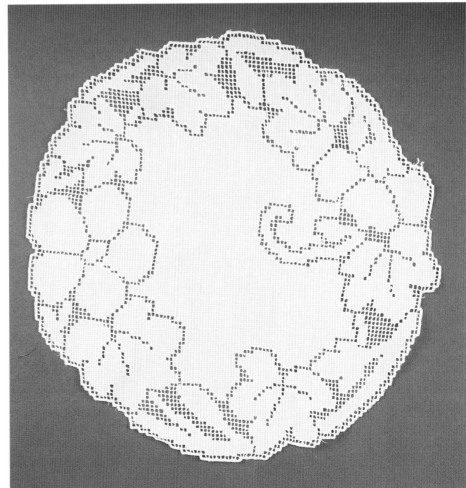

Punchwork - Italy, 16" round, stiletto
punched holes kept open by hand
overcast buttonhole stitches on linen,
poor imitations are made in China, c.
1910-1940, each $15-20.

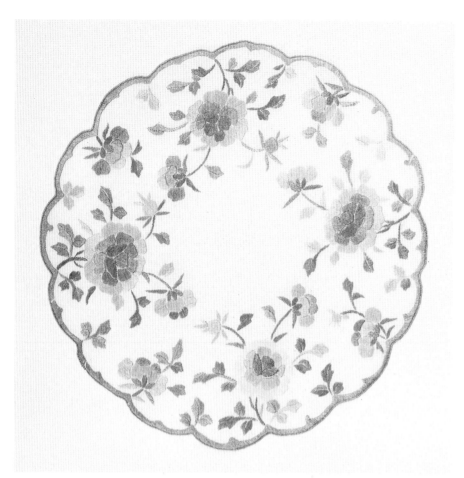

Rice Cloth - China, up to 18", the cloth is made from the nettle plant and the silk floss is expertly hand embroidered Oriental patterns, c. 1900-1960, $10-25.

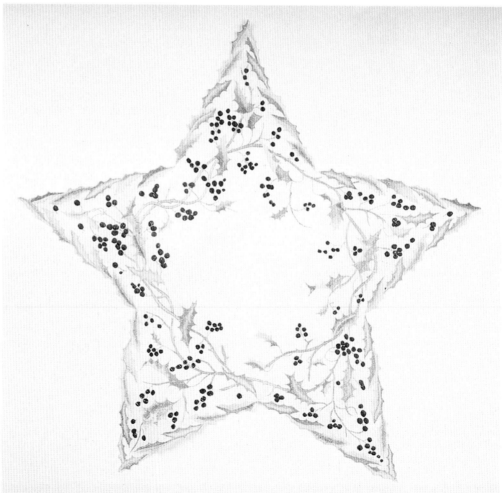

Silk Embroidery - America, up to 18", silk floss hand embroidery on fine linen, c. 1870-1915, $40-75.

Society Silk Embroidery -
America, up to 18",
exquisite silk floss hand
embroidery on fine linen
made only by accom-
plished women of wealth,
c. 1870-1925, $50-100.

Also available:

Alençon - France, up to 18", machine made lace with a delicate cream mesh ground and a hand run needle lace design outlined with cordonnets, c. 1890-1985, $15-35.

Needle Lace - Belgium/Italy, 9" round, used as an under plate doily with white, cream, or taupe embroidery threads, c. 1880-1955, each $10-12.

Normandy Lace - France, 12" round, hand assembled multiple patchwork of white or cream Paris Lace with a handmade embroidered lace center, c. 1900-1950, each $25-45.

Tambour - Switzerland, 8" round, white
cotton with tambour chain stitching used
as underplates, c. 1900-1950, $10 each.

Doily 63

DOILY PRESS - a matched pair of fabric covered rounds used to keep sets of doilies in place and neatly tied together with a silk ribbon.

Doily Press - America, up to 18" round, cotton or linen floral fabric with silk ribbon ties, c. 1880-1950, pair $15-25.

Doylies Press - United Kingdom, any size square, silk embroidery on linen with paper pages inside for flat pressing, c. 1900-1950, $20-30.

Also available:

Placemat Press - America, 22"L x 18"W, printed cardboard bottom with a clear vinyl top held together with fabric covered elastics, c. 1915-1955, $20-25.

DUVET COVERS - European fabric covers used to protect feather down comforters and blankets. In Europe, each person had his or her own personal feather content comforter, thus the small width size.

Cotton - America, 90"L x 82"W, two pieces of white cotton sewn together on all four sides with a center opening about 12"-18" surrounded by fancy embroidery, c. 1880-1940, $35-45; pair of twins $45-55.

Linen - Eastern Europe, 78"L x 56"W, a flat top cover with hand embroidery, cutwork, lace, and/or monograms with buttonholes on the other three sides for buttoning onto the comforter or blanket, c. 1880-1950, $50-75.

Printed Fabric - Eastern Europe, 88"L x 68"W, floral, checkered, or geometric patterned cotton or linen fabric for buttoning onto the comforter or blanket, c. 1880-1980, $50-75.

EGG COZY - Half moon shaped back-to-back fabric covers for keeping soft boiled eggs hot. These are quite unique and are a rare find.

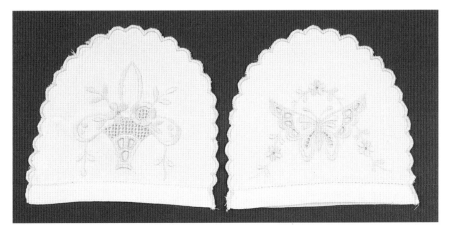

Also available:

Cotton - America, 4"H x 3"W, quilted cotton fabric, c. 1900-1970, each $5.

Crochet - Scotland, 3.75"H x 2.75"W, heavy white cotton crochet thread, c. 1920-1960, each $5.

Linen - United Kingdom, 4"H x 3"W, light blue machine stitched embroidery, c. 1880-1970, each $10.

GLASS SLIPPERS - Two pieces of fabric sewn together with a slit in the center. These are still practical and are conversation pieces. These slippers fit the bottom of stemware to prevent water rings on furniture as the liquid in the glass forms condensation.

Roosters, elephants, and fancy embroidery - Portugal, 3" round or square hand embroidered, c. 1915-1965, each $5.

Also available:

Lace - China, 3" round or square, handmade needle lace made with ivory or white cotton thread, c. 1920-1980, $5 each.

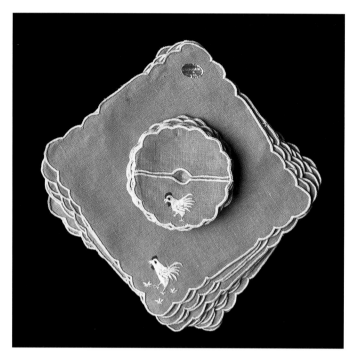

Linen - Madeira, 3" round slippers with matching 6"L x 6"W cocktail napkins, c. 1915-1965, set of six, $55-75.

GLOVE BAG - Pretty rectangular linen keepers for a lady's everyday necessity.

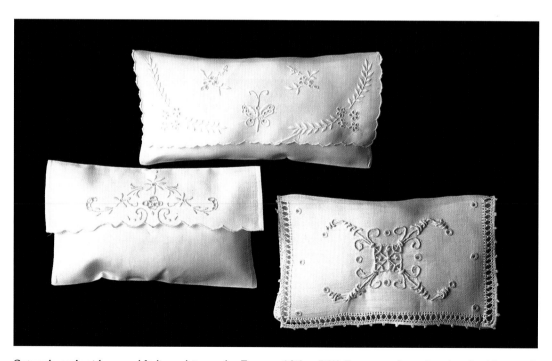

Cutwork, embroidery, and Italian white work - Europe, 10"L x 5"W, European fancy hand embroidery and cutwork on crisp linen, c. 1870-1945, each $20-30.

Embroidery - America, 10"L x 5"W, lovely colored silk hand embroidery on linen or cotton, c. 1870-1955, $25-35.

HANDKERCHIEF ENVELOPES - Usually square, these handy organizers keep small articles together.

Cutwork - France, square, French embroidery, cutwork, lace, and satin linings all on linen, c. 1880-1940, each $25-45.

Lace - France, 6"L x 6"W, delicate needle run pattern on fine net background with a padded silk fabric liner, c. 1880-1950, $35-55.

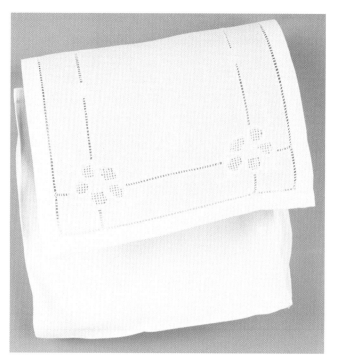

Linen - England, 6"L x 6"W, hemstitching, drawnwork, with or without lace, and often with an embroidered monogram on linen, c. 1880-1950, $20-30.

HOT FOOD COVERS - These fabric covers, shaped with four wings, were specifically made to be wrapped around prepared foods to keep them hot. The most often found embroidered food covers are: "BAKED POTATOES, BAGELS, CORN, HOT BISCUITS, HOT ROLLS, MUFFINS, SANDWICHES, TOAST," and "TORTILLAS." Either cotton or linen fabric was used.

Hot Biscuits, Bagels, Hot Corn, Hot Roll, and Toast - Portugal, 18"L x 18"W, white or cream linen with hand embroidery in white, light blue, or taupe floss, c. 1930-1960, each $15-25.

Hot Rolls - United Kingdom, 22"L x 22"W, white Irish linen with a filet crochet lace insert "HOT ROLLS MAKE THE [BUTTERFLY]," c. 1920-1960, $20-35.

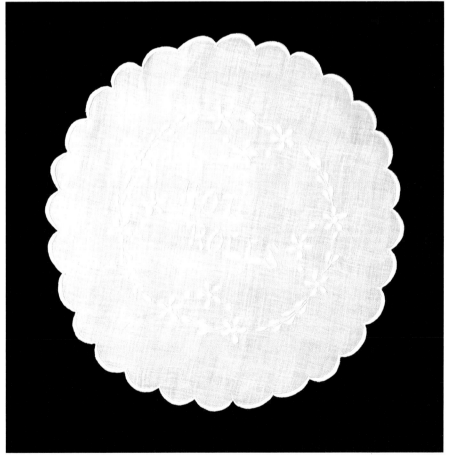

Hot Rolls - Portugal, 18" round, white embroidery of Hot Rolls on white linen for the bottom of the roll basket, c. 1930-1960, $15-25.

Sandwiches - America, 17"L x 17" W, white linen with cross stitched "SANDWICHES" and a design, c. 1930-1950, $15-25.

HOT PLATES - These are heavily crocheted decorative doilies often with asbestos or metal liners to keep hot dishes from scorching surfaces.

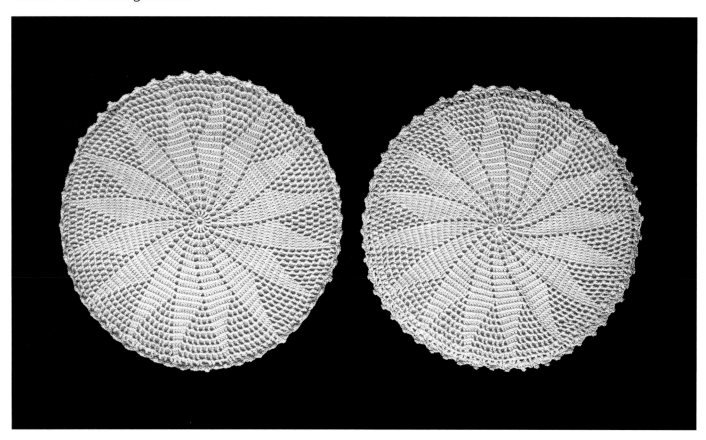

Crochet - America, 6"-12" round, tightly crocheted mats made to fit snugly around asbestos plates, c. 1920-1950, $10-20.

Crochet - America, 6"-16" round, heavy crochet over metal bottle caps in clusters of cherries or grapes, c. 1930-1950, $15-25.

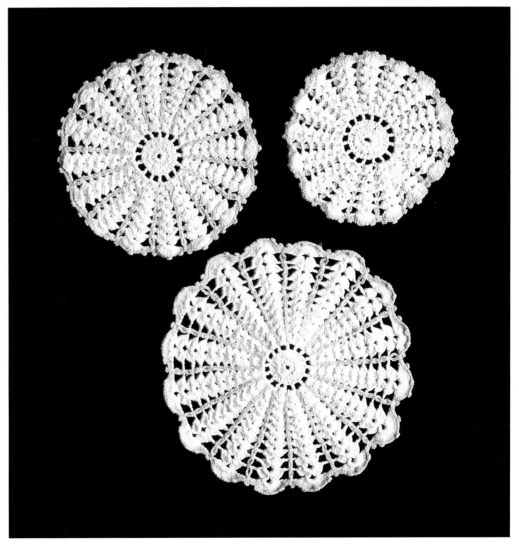

Crochet - America, any size or shape, made of heavy, tight lace, c. 1920-1950, $10.

Crochet - America, any size or shape, made of heavy, tight lace, c. 1920-1950, $10.

HOT WATER BOTTLE COVER - A decorative cover to hide a very utilitarian item.

Linen - America, 10"H x 8"W, hand cross stitched "HOT WATER," c. 1900-1940, $15-25.

LAMP SHADE COVER - Decorative shade covers for wall sconces or single candleholders. Not too many exist because of fire damage.

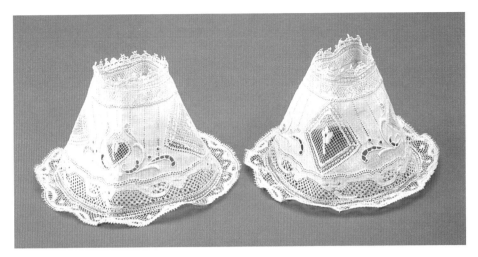

Linen - France/Italy, 7"H x 6"W, cone shaped cream linen with net lace insertions, Paris Lace edging, cutwork, and embroidery, c. 1880-1940, each $150-200.

LAUNDRY BAG - Decorative bags to transport soiled laundry to the laundry service when washing facilities were not available at home.

Muslin - America, 20"L x 16"W, possibly made from a kit, "LAUNDRY" hand embroidered with whimsical appliqués, c. 1880-1940, $50-60. *Courtesy of Maria Arata.*

LINEN ROLL - Long, fabric decorated tube to use as a linen press, often with layers of tissue paper inside.

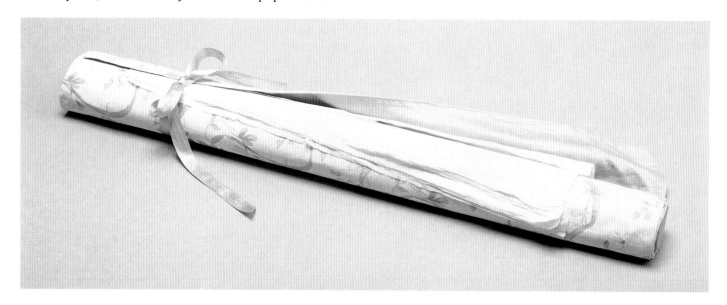

Linen - America, 36"L, floral fabric covering many sheets of tissue paper inside with a silk ribbon closure, c. 1890-1950, $40-50.

LINGERIE ENVELOPE - Decorative fabric envelopes for storing nightwear in the bedroom during the day. We now use them as boudoir decorations with feather pillow forms inside.

Good Night - England, 18"L x 15"W, white filet crochet with a linen back, c. 1890-1950, $55-75. *Courtesy of Anna from The Old Lace and Linen Shop, Inc.*

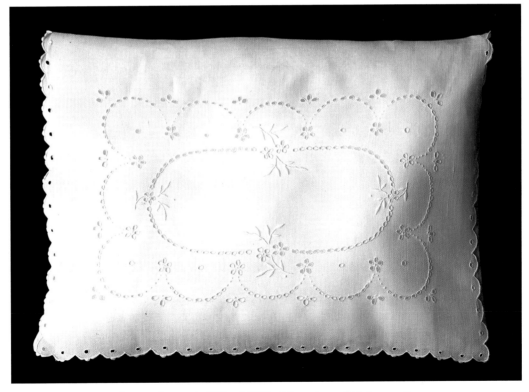

Linen - Portugal, 18"L x 15"W, white or ivory Irish linen with Madeira hand embroidery, c. 1900-1950, $45-65.

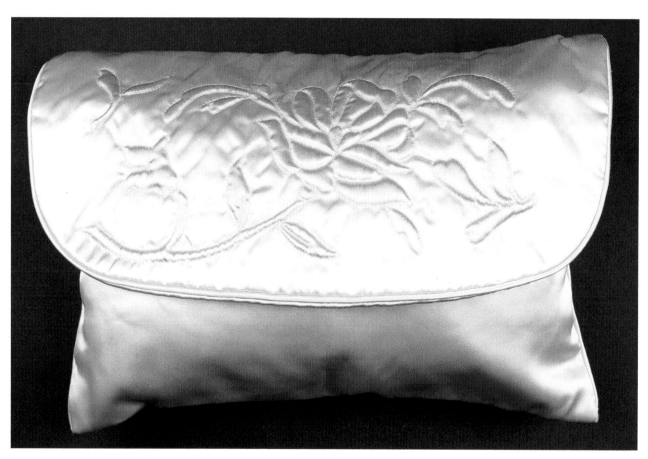

Satin - America, 16"L x 11"W, pastel colored satin with quilted designs often with other matching pieces used during traveling, c. 1915-1945, $20-30.

Silk embroidery - Great Britain, 19"L x 16"W, hand embroidery in cotton or silk on crisp Irish linen, c. 1900-1950, $45-65. *Courtesy of Janice Liljestrand.*

Turkey Redwork - America, 14"L x 12"W, muslin cotton with "NIGHT DRESS" embroidered in turkey redwork made from the bright red yolks of turkey eggs, c. 1870-1900, $65-85.

MANTLE SCARF - A custom made piece specifically designed to fit a certain mantle. These are hard to find to exactly fit your mantle.

Linen - America, 66"L x 6"W, natural flax linen with drawnwork and flax tassels in between hand crocheted fans, c. 1930-1945, $45-55.

MARGHAB LINENS - Vera Way Marghab and her husband Emile, founded the Marghab Linen Company in Funchal, Portugal, in 1934 and produced linens until 1978. Vera was the designer of most of the three hundred patterns with the assistance of her brother-in-law, Theo. Marghab Linens were specifically made to satisfy the most discerning customer being sold only in the finest salons and exclusive shops. Only a few selected, patiently trained peasants, who worked out of their homes, were permitted to be a Marghab embroideress. It was a true cottage industry. The embroidery artists worked on pieces that could take up to one month to create and held as many as 85,000 stitches. The fabrics were all hand selected and produced only in Ireland and Switzerland to Vera's specifications. Marghab Linens are known worldwide as the perfect gift because of their quality, workmanship, and design. Many gifts of Marghab Linens can still be found today in their original boxes with their original tags, still waiting for that special day to use them.

Cocktail Napkins - Portugal, 7"L x 4"W, fine linen with all hand embroidery
made by the Marghab Company, c. 1934-1978, each $20-30.

Cocktail Napkins - Portugal, 8"L x 5"W, from their *Under The Sea* series, comes these little teal colored fish and coral colored seaweed in fine white Irish linen in their original box, c. 1934-1978, each $25-35.

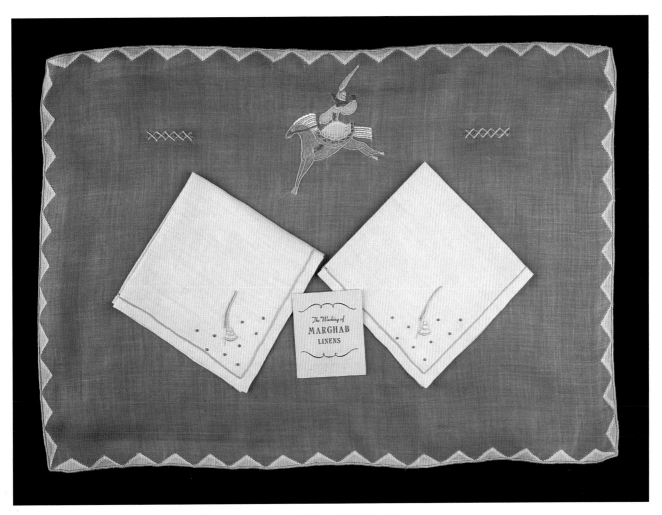

Tea For Two - Portugal, 22"L x 16"W, Varishka or any pattern with two matching napkins, c. 1934-1978, set $150-250.

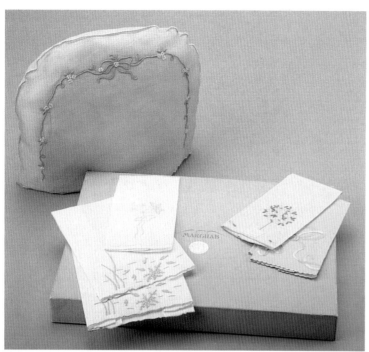

Tea Cozy - Portugal, 14"H x 12"W, Swiss Margandie fabric with a padded cotton liner in the Victoria pattern, c. 1934-1978, $150-250.

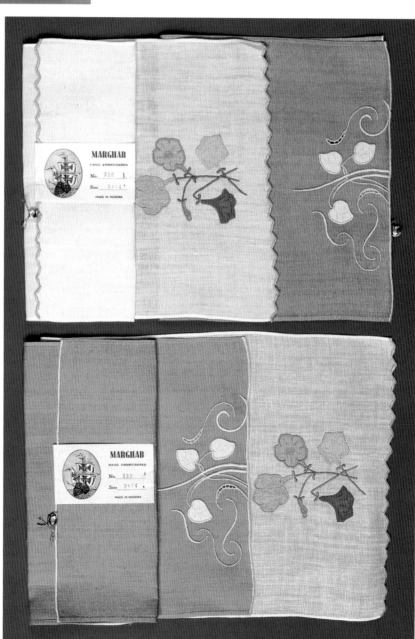

Towel - Portugal, 14"L x 9"W, four guest fingertip towels each with their original pinned on paper labels and metal Madeira identification tags, c. 1934-1978, each $75-125.

Towel - Portugal, 21"L x 15"W, three Marghab Jacaranda Tree
pattern guest towels in various colors, c. 1934-1978, each $50-75.

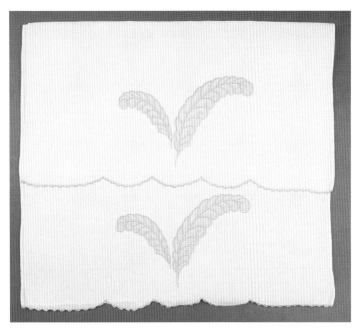

Towel - Portugal, 14"L x 9"W, two Plume pattern guest fingertip towels in Irish linen with appliqués, c. 1934-1978, pair $50-100.

Also available:

Baby Sheet and Pillowcase - Portugal, any size, in the rare Birdlings pattern, c. 1934-1978, set $100-250.

Biscuit Cover - Portugal, 18"L x 18"W, white or natural Irish linen in the Vignette pattern, c. 1934-1978, $75-145.

Dinner Cloth - Portugal, any size, any pattern, with matching napkins, c. 1934-1978, from $200 on up.

Goblet Rounds - Portugal, 5", any pattern, c. 1934-1978, each $25-35.

Placemat and Napkin Set - Portugal, 18"L x 12"W, one placemat and one napkin that can take up to four weeks to embroider, c. 1934-1978, set $75-125.

Tea Cloth and Napkin Set - Portugal, 36"L x 36"W, in any pattern with a set of 13"L x 13"W napkins, c. 1934-1978, set $150-300.

MODESTY WEDDING SHEET - Made specifically for a young woman's trousseau, this fancy embroidered, cutwork, and often monogrammed white sheet had a slit in the very center for the modest bride on her wedding night.

Linen - Europe, 110"L x 90"W, white Irish linen for moral purity, c. 1840-1915, $50-75.

Also available:

Damask Linen - Europe, 98"L x 88"W, floral pattern on white linen damask, c. 1860-1915, $50-75.

NAPKIN - Civilized dining requires a proper table set with an individual napkin to be placed on your lap. Previous etiquette dictated tying the napkin around your neck. A napkin larger than 26" is considered a lapkin so they can then be used for buffet serving and table dining. Some large napkins can be found with a buttonhole in one corner to be buttoned to the top button of a shirt.

Cocktail - America, 8"L x 8"W, cheerful slogans printed on linen, c. 1925-1965, each $5-8.

Cocktail - Portugal, Switzerland, and France, all about 10"L x 5"W, all with hand embroidery on linen, c. 1925-1965, each $8-10.

Cocktail - France, 8"L x 8"W, linen with white embroidery "CHAM-PAGNE," c. 1920-1960, each $7-10.

Cocktail - Portugal, 8"L x 5"W, made exclusively for Constance Leiter, Inc., eight mushroom pattern napkins on linen, quite possibly the next serious collectible, c. 1940-1970, each $10-12.

Cocktail - Portugal, 7"L x 5"W, risqué or naughty napkins of four happy men.

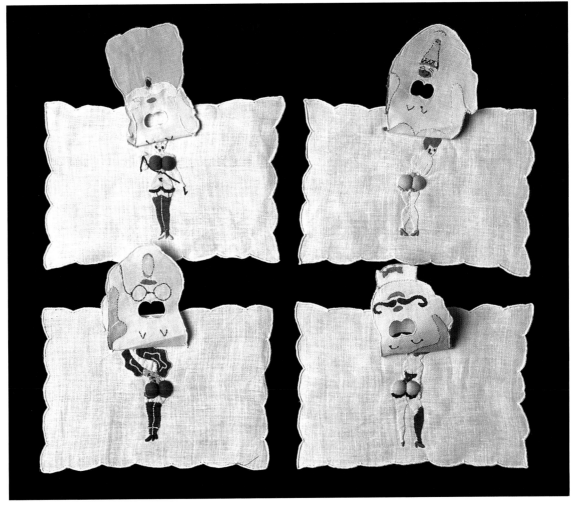

Cocktail - Portugal, 7"L x 5"W, after lifting the happy men's faces, there appears four risqué ladies! All hand embroidered on linen, c. 1935-1965, each $15-25.

Cocktail – Portugal, all about 7"L x 5"W, risqué ladies that are embroidered,
appliquéd, seen through a keyhole, and bearing all! C. 1935-1965, each $15-25.

Dinner - European, all about 18-20"L x 18-20"W, an assortment of white and ivory linen dinner napkins with cutwork, embroidery, lace, appliqué, and punchwork, c. 1920-1950, each $5-7.

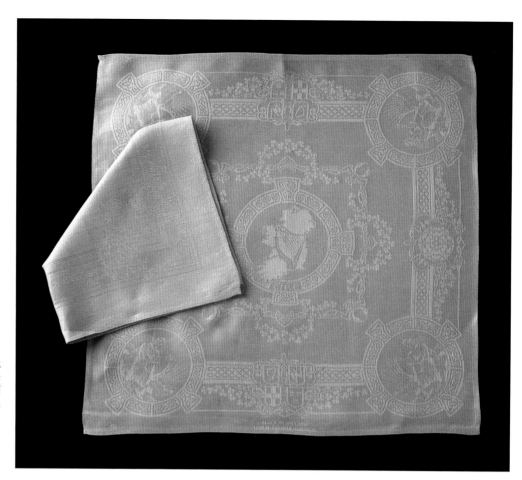

Dinner - Ireland, from 17"L x 17"W up to 25"L x 25"W, fine "MADE IN IRELAND LINEN DOUBLE DAMASK" woven into the pattern in colored linen, c. 1925-1975, each $10-15.

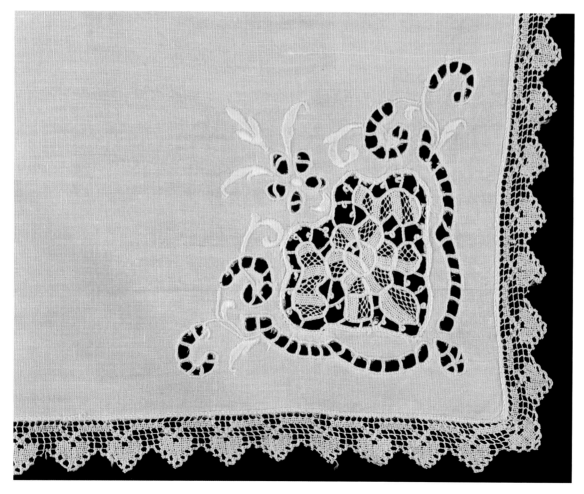

Dinner - Italy, from 17"L x 17"W up to 24"L x 24"W, white or ecru linen, with or without lace edge, and one corner with cutwork, embroidery, and a lace insertion, c.1890-1980, each $10-12.

Dinner - Portugal, from 17"L x 17"W up to 24"L x 24"W, fine woven linen with cutwork, embroidery, lace in one corner, and a scalloped edge, c. 1930-1980, each $8-12.

Below:
Dinner - United Kingdom, from 17"L x 17"W up to 24"L x 24"W, stately linen with a double damask pattern in either floral or geometric pattern, c. 1860-1970, each $10-15; animal, figural, mythological scenes, or Celtic locations, each $15-20; hand painted flowers, each $12-15.

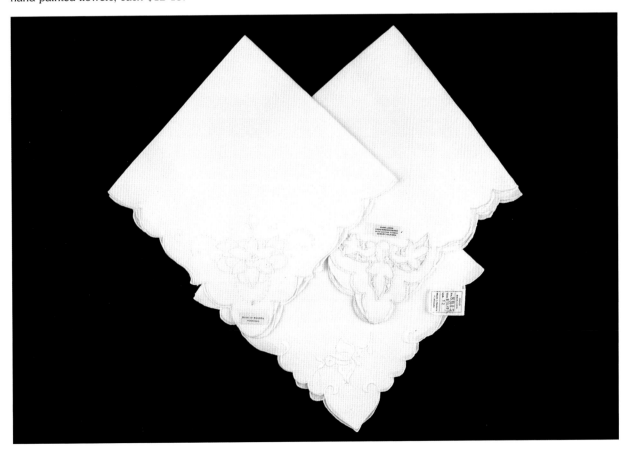

Finger Bowl - China, 9"L x 6"W, with cutwork, embroidery, and typical straight Chinese drawnwork in sets of six, c. 1920-1970, each $5-7.

Below:
Luncheon - Belgium, from 14" up to 18" square, slightly smaller than dinner napkins, usually with a row of drawnwork on double damask patterned linen, c. 1900-1960, each $5-7.

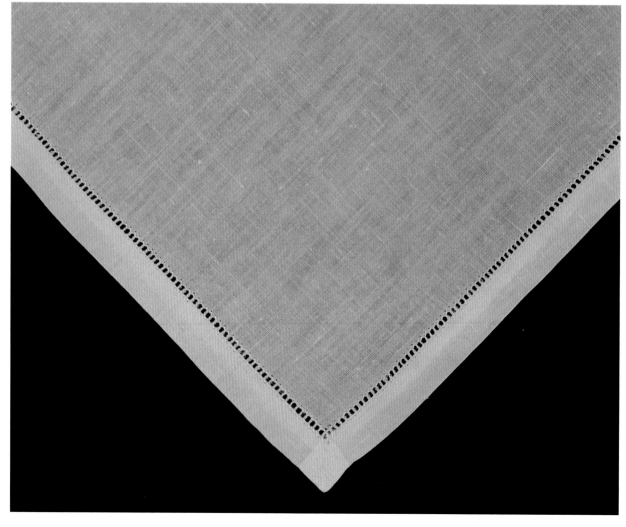

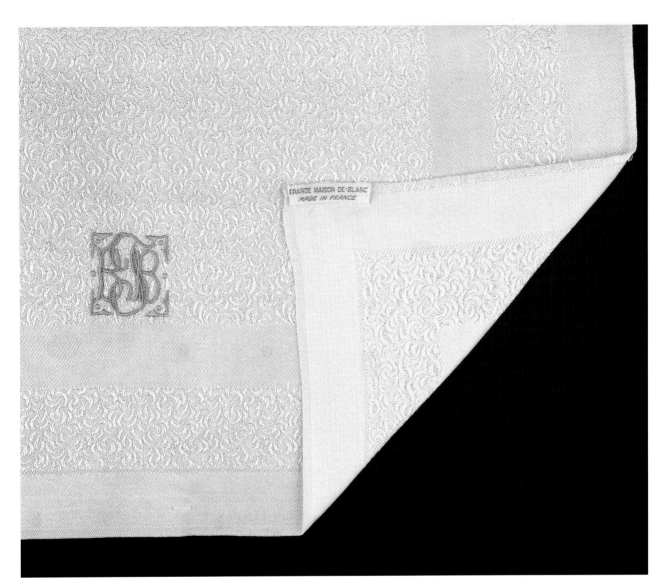

Rayon - France, 24"L x 24"W, soft pearl gray or any pastel color, hand embroidered intricate monogram, hand stitched hems, and a fabric label indicating its origin, c. 1900-1960, each $12-15.

Tea - Eastern Europe, from 10"-13"L x 10"-13"W, used for tea, dessert, or cocktails, these are small but adequate, mostly made of imported fine woven Irish linen with tailored or fancy embellishments, c. 1900-1955, each $4-6.

Left and below:
Tea for Two - Eastern Europe, any size, this set can be one or two placemats with two napkins and always fancy for entertaining, c. 1900-1955, set $25-35.

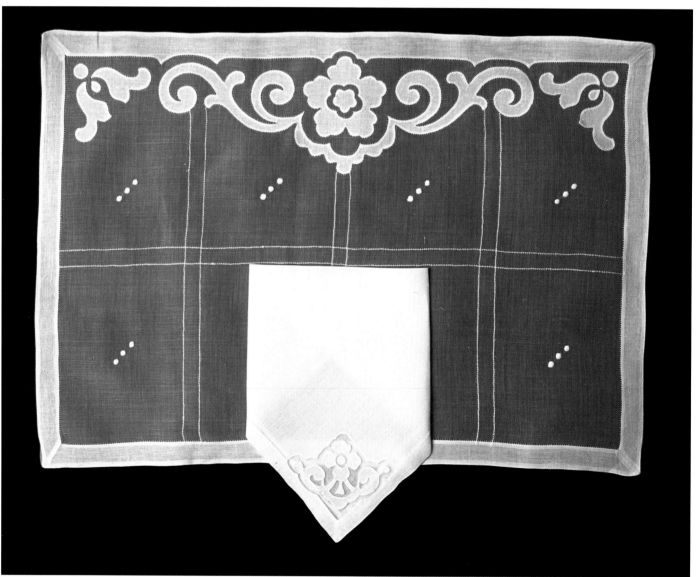

Also available:

Lapkin - Belgium, 26"-36"L x 20"-32"W, double damask floral and scroll pattern, c. 1880-1950, each $12-15; hand stitched hems with lace and a monogram, each $14-17; figural double damask pattern, each $17-20.

Lapkin - United Kingdom, from 26" up to 36" square, any floral or geometric pattern mostly with hand stitched hems and an intricate monogram, c. 1860-1950, each $15-20; figural pattern, each $20-25.

Rectangular - Eastern Europe, from 36"L to 32"W, fabric can be patterned damask or fine woven linen, hand stitched hems, with or without lace, embroidery, cutwork, or monograms, c. 1880-1950, each $15-20.

Tea - Portugal, 11"L x 11"W, crisp white Irish linen purchased at a specialty linen shop with Madeira white or blue hand embroidery in the butterfly, basket, or urn pattern, c. 1900-1960, each $5-8.

NAPKIN RINGS - These scarce pieces are considered personal items. Napkins were used three times a day for many days thus different patterns were used on the rings to differentiate one's own napkin from someone else's napkin. Often the napkin rings were taken along when one moved away from home hence, the difficulty of finding complete sets.

Ring - America, 9"L x 1"W, cotton crochet, c. 1900-1940, set of six, $24-36.

Ring - America, 7"L x 1.5"W, embroidery on linen, tat lace edge,
and a snap closure, c. 1900-1950, each $6-8.

Ring - Italian, 8"L x 3"W, hand embroidery, needle lace, and button closure
on linen with matching napkin set wrap, c. 1900-1950, set $50-60.

NAPKIN WRAPS - These nifty items were purchased in kit form and are meant to keep sets of napkins together. Some wraps have companion utensil and table-cloth holders.

Wrap - America, 18"L x 18"W with four sides to neatly wrap around the napkins, in any fabric with a closure, c. 1900-1950, $15-25.

Wrap - America, 12"L x 3"W, cross stitched "NAPKINS" on fabric with a tie, c. 1900-1950, $10-15.

Wrap - America, 20"L x 12"W, felt lined cream linen cover made from a kit with "NAPKINS" hand embroidered, c. 1910-1940, $15-25.

PARASOL/WALKING STICK HOLDER - Interesting storage case kept by the front door; often held necessity or vanity items.

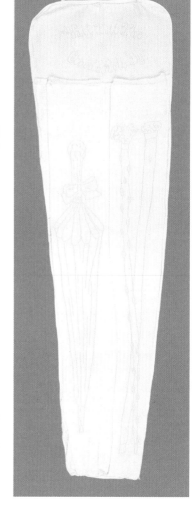

Holder - America, 42"L x 9"W, a two compartment holder made with heavy cotton canvas and hand embroidery, c. 1885-1915, $45-75.

PIANO SCARF - When cashmere paisley printed shoulder mantles and silk embroidered square shawls with long fringe fell out of fashion around 1890, these were relegated to the piano. These piano scarves are now being reused as shawls once again. Please refer to *Victorian Paisley Shawls* by Chet Gadsby (Schiffer Publishing Ltd, 2002).

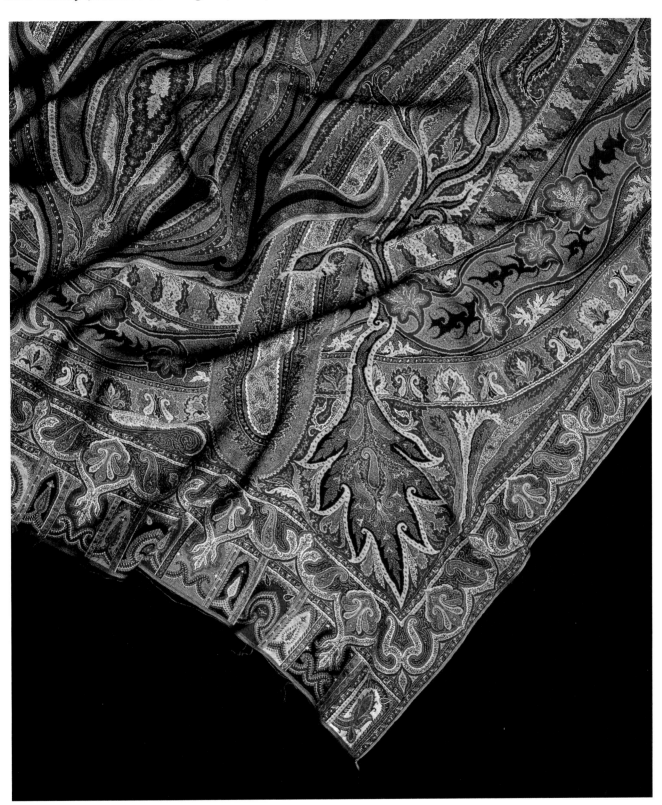

Paisley Shawl - Scotland/France/Central Europe - Made of cashmere/wool/silk in various patterns, colors, and sizes, c. 1820-1875, $75-2,500.

PILLOW SHAMS - A sham is a cover up. Originally, flat top shams were used to lay over wrinkled pillowcases during the day and were to be taken off at night. Later shams were highly decorative and were to show off one's needle skills. European shams are 18" to 36" square. American shams are 26" to 36" long and are rectangular. Decorative shams for the boudoir are round, square, oval, oblong, rectangular, or heart shaped.

Envelope - America, 24"W x 28"L, a pillow is to be inserted from the top with a front v-shaped closure, c. 1880-1950, each $45-65.

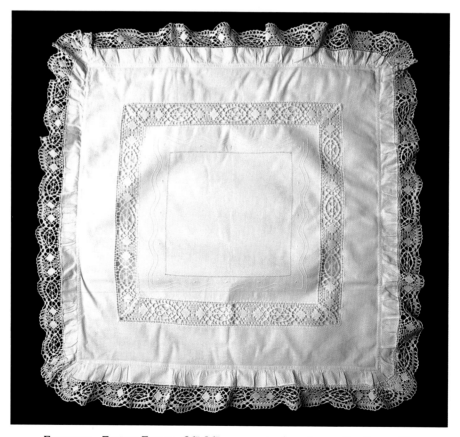

European - Eastern Europe, 26"-36" square, sturdy cotton or fine linen with a button closure in the back, usually very decorative with ruffles, cutwork, embroidery, and a monogram, c. 1880-1980, each $75-125.

Turkey Redwork - America, 24"-36" square or rectangular with Turkey redwork
embroidery of bedtime sayings, monograms, birds, or scroll patterns, often
with many rows of tucks and ruffles, c. 1860-1920, pair $100-150.

Filet Crochet - America/Europe, 26"-36" square or rectangle, companions to filet crochet bedspreads, c. 1920-1950, pair $55-75.

Italian - about 30"L x 20"W, cotton shams with broderie anglaise-type eyelet lace on the front with cotton ties to secure the pillow inside, c. 1880-1940, pair $50-75.

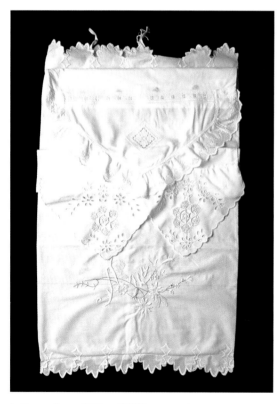

Italian - about 30"L x 20"W, cotton shams, top one with lace insert, satin ribbon, and ruffle. Middle sham with hand cutwork. Bottom sham from a wedding trousseau with "AMORE" hand embroidered, c. 1880-1940, pair $50-75.

Also available:

Layover - America, 24"-36" square or rectangular with white tambour stitching in a scroll pattern, monograms, rows of tucks, ruffles, or bedtime sayings, c. 1860-1920, each $50-75.

PILLOWCASE WRAP - Made from a pre-stamped kit, wraps also can have other linen closet companions such as sheets, blanket covers, and towels.

Wrap - America, 12"L x 3"W, cross stitched "PILLOW CASES" on fabric to keep a set of pillowcases neatly together in the linen press, c. 1900-1950, $10-15.

PILLOWCASES - Often called pillow slips, these traditional tailored or decorative everyday household items are used to protect the feather or foam pillow from having to be washed often. Standard American pillows are 26"L x 20"W, queen 30"L x 20"W, and king 36"L x 20"W.

Appenzell - Switzerland, 32"L x 24"W, always on high count linen fabric with the finest hand embroidery mostly of figures, c. 1900-1960, pair $150-250; floral, pair $100-200.

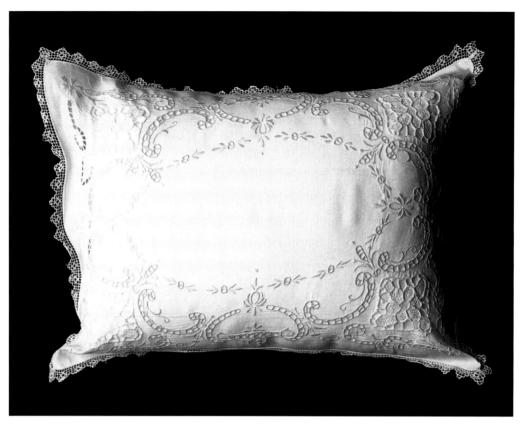

Baby - Italy, 18"L x 15"W, linen with light blue hand embroidery, cutwork, lace insertions, and filet Rose lace around the edge, c. 1900-1950, $45-65; figural $75-125.

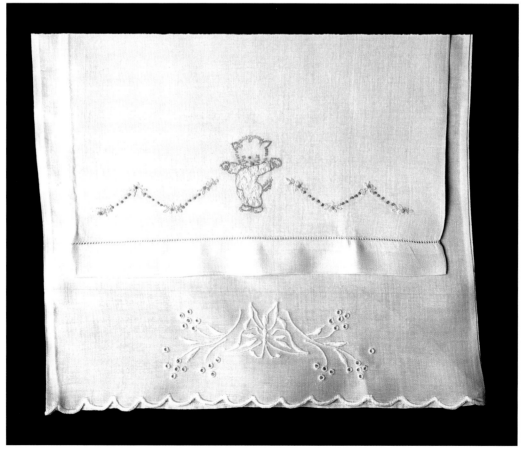

Baby - Portugal, 18"L x 12"W, both hand embroidered on fine linen with hand stitched seams, c. 1900-1950, each $20-40.

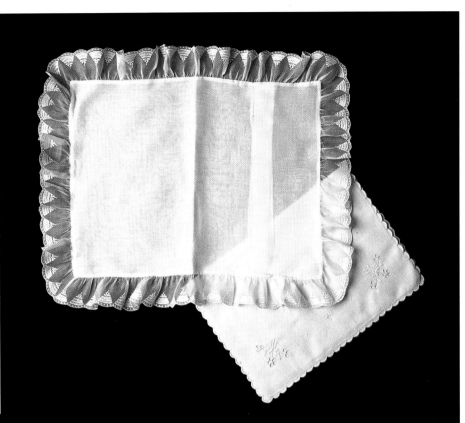

Baby - Switzerland, 16"L x 12"W, fine cotton organdy in all its gossamer glory with fancy work and a ruffled or scalloped edge, c. 1900-1965, $25-45.

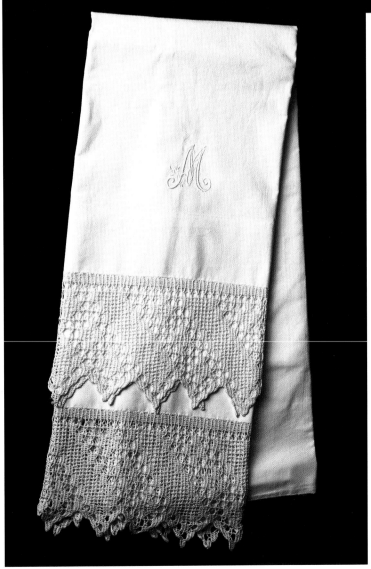

Cotton - America, 28"-34"L x 18"-22"W, muslin or percale cotton with an original paper label and a plain machine stitched hem, c. 1890-1970, pair $15-30; with added deep crochet lace 2"+, pair $35-65.

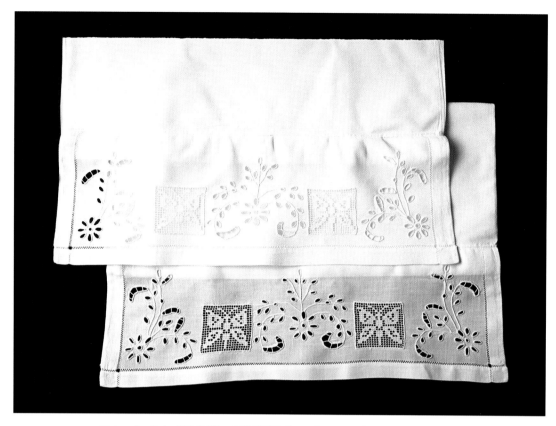

Cutwork - Italy, 30"-34"L x 18"-22"W, fine white percale cotton with hand cutwork and embroidery, often with a paper label or ink printed "MADE IN ITALY" that are meant specifically for export, c. 1930-1960, pair $45-75.

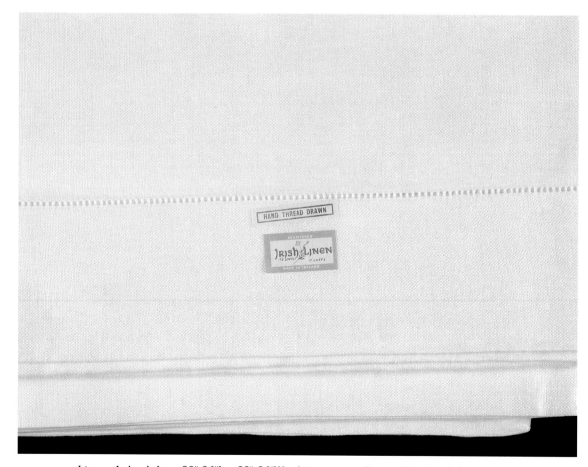

Linen - Ireland, from 30"-36"L x 22"-26"W, white or cream linen with a hand drawn thread hem, with or without embellishments, c. 1900-present, pair $30-90.

Embroidered - America, from 28"-36"L x 18"-26"W, mostly made from a pre-stamped kit with either a cross stitch or embroidery design, pretty floss, and often with a lace edge, c. 1900-1970, cotton pair $25-65; linen pair $65-100.

Southern Belle and pre-stamped - America, from 28"-34"L x 18"-22"W, both pre-stamped
pattern on cotton muslin with added ruffle or crochet lace, c. 1930-1970, pair $25-75.

Madeira - Portugal, from 30"-36"L x 18"-22"W, famous light blue or white hand embroidery and cutwork, c. 1900-1970, cotton pair $25-75; linen pair $75-100.

Also available:

Bolster - America, 66"L x 22"W, tube-shaped seamless fabric for one long cylindrical pillow or two flat rectangular pillows, can be cut in half to make two pillowcases, c. 1880-1965, cotton $25-35; linen $45-85.

Bolster - Europe, 78"L x 24"W, mostly linen or cotton tube-shaped seamless fabric for one long cylindrical pillow with either cutwork, embroidery, lace, or monograms. These can still be purchased in Europe and used with modern body pillows, c. 1860-present, cotton $35-55; linen $55-85.

China - 32"L x 22"W, mostly cotton, occasionally linen, with predominantly light blue or white embroidery with some cutwork, c. 1925-present, pair $15-30; linen pair $30-50.

Homespun - America/Europe, from 20"-40"L x 16"-22"W, cream linen with hand stitched seams often with a red cross stitched monogram and a number that was meant for rotation purposes (since women acquired their lifetime collection of household linen from their trousseau, it was necessary to rotate their use to ensure equal wear), c. 1850-1910, pair $45-75.

Linen - Italy, 30"-34"L x 20"-26"W, cream linen with hand embroidery, cutwork, and "BUON RIPOSO, BUONO NOTTI, FELICITA," or "BUON GIORNO," c. 1880-1980, $75-100.

Monogrammed - America/Europe, from 28"-40"L x 18"-26"W, mostly with satin padded hand embroidery, c. 1880-1980, cotton pair $35-65; linen pair $65-95.

Square - Eastern Europe, 26"-36" square, button back closure, lace insertion, edging, and a monogram, c. 1900-1980, cotton pair $75-125; linen $125-175.

PIN CUSHION - When needlework was a fashionable parlor art for women's afternoon gatherings, a lady would use her fancy whitework cushion while her utilitarian red tomato cushion would be relegated to the common sewing basket.

Round - America, from 5"-8", two pieces of embroidered and cutwork linen are to hold a tightly packed sawdust filled cushion all tied together with a ribbon, c. 1890-1940, $20-40.

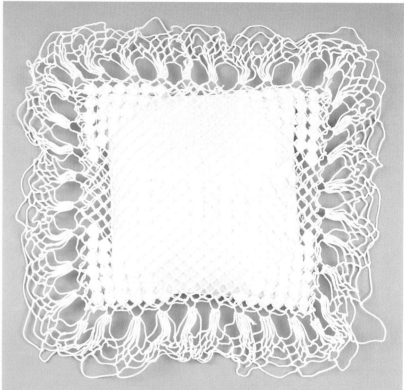

Square - Armenia, from 6"-12", cotton Armenian Lace custom made to snugly fit around a satin cushion filled with pumice for needle sharpening, c. 1900-1940, $15-25.

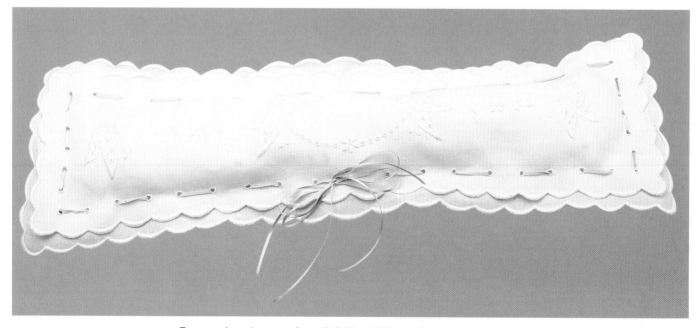

Rectangular - America, from 6"-24"L x 8"W, pre-stamped linen from a kit complete with a firm rubber-type cushion, c. 1880-1940, $20-60.

PLACEMATS - Used to take the place of a tablecloth, individual placemats and matching napkins were used. Dinner sets consist of twelve placemats, twelve napkins, twelve glass coasters, and one or two center runners in any shape.

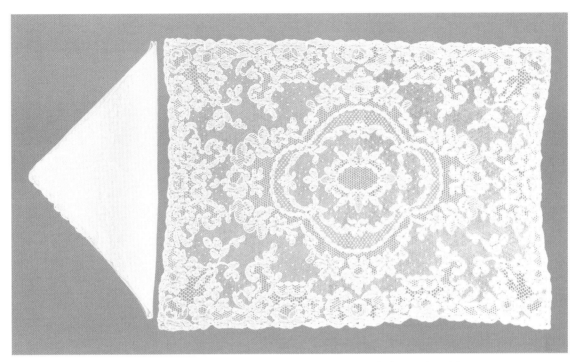

Alençon - France, 16"L x 13"W, cream colored machine made lace with a delicate mesh ground, outlined with cordonnet cording, and linked with brides without picots, c. 1890-1985, each $35-45; with matching linen and lace napkin, add $25-35.

Appenzell - Switzerland, 14"L x 11"W, fine white linen with a lacy confection of exceptional embroidery of women with Buratto lattice work, c. 1890-1960, each $50-75; fancy work without figures, $25-50; with a matching napkin add $25.

Chemical Lace - Germany, 16"L x 14"W, fancy Plauen Lace on netting with a chemically removed ground in ivory or white, c. 1880-1940, each $10-15.

Figural - Italy, 16" round, fine ivory or white linen with net lace inserts, edging, cutwork, and embroidery, c. 1880-1970, each $20-30.
Courtesy of Snow Leopard Antiques.

Lace - France, about 16"L x 12"W and 15" round, French Normandy lace, Alençon lace, and Point de France lace, all ivory, c. 1900-1970, each $15-25; with matching linen napkin, $25-50.

Linen - Italy, all about 16"L x 12"W, all linen with various handmade laces, embroidery, punchwork, and cutwork, c. 1900-1970, each $15-25; with matching linen napkin, $25-50.

Linen - Madeira, Portugal, all about 16"L x 12"W, all linen with various handmade laces, embroidery, cutwork, and appliqués, c. 1900-1970, each $15-25; with matching linen napkin, $25-50.

Luncheon - Portugal, 14"L x 12"W, crisp Irish linen with Madeira blue embroidery, four napkins, center runner, and a biscuit cover, c. 1900-1960, set $125-175.

Net Darning - China, 14"L x 11"W, white or ivory mesh background with a needle run floral, figural, or geometric pattern, c. 1920-1960, each $10-20; with a matching napkin, set $25-35.

Organdy - Portugal, 14"L x 11"W, any color of fine woven gossamer cotton with cutwork, embroidery, lace, and appliqués with a matching napkin, c. 1925-1980, $20-35.

Also available:

Needle Lace - China, 16"L x 12"W, ecru cotton thread with an acorn pattern, c. 1910-1960, each $10; with a matching linen center lace edged napkin, set $25-35.

POT HOLDERS - Since early cookware was cast iron, potholders were a necessity. To add decoration to an everyday mundane item, quilted holders in early calico fabrics were made and are now highly prized treasures.

Crochet - America, thick cotton lace in any size, c. 1880-present, each $5-10.

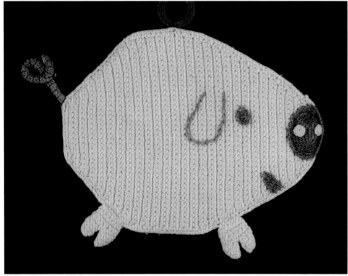

Crochet - America, whimsical pink pig, c. 1940s, $25-45.

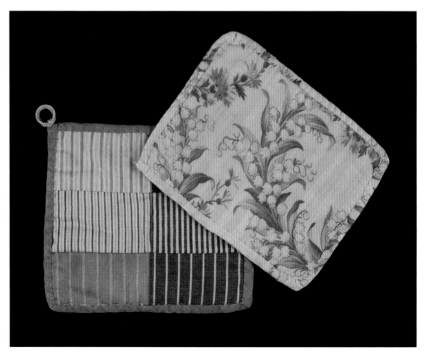

Fabric - America, early hand quilted calico fabric with cotton batting inside, c. 1840-1920, $25-75.

Set - America, cotton muslin with hand embroidery from a kit, possibly made as a gift, c. 1910-1940, set $15-25.

Also available:

Knit - America, thick cotton lace in any size, c. 1880-present, each $5-10.

ROUND TABLECLOTHS - Since doilies stop at 18", round tablecloths can often be as large as 150".

Appenzell - Switzerland, 54" round, white linen decorated with the finest hand embroidery, c. 1880-1970, $125-175.

Chemical Lace - Germany, 36" round, Plauen Lace made of sturdy white cotton to resemble old world lace without the cost, c. 1870-1940, $50-75; 48" round, $75-125; 60" round, $125-200; 72" round, $200-300.

Cluny Lace - France, 36" round, a continuous bobbin lace with a linen center of net filet inserts, cutwork, and embroidery, c. 1880-present, $75-125; 48" round, $125-175; 60" round, $175-225; 72" round, $225-275; 84" round, $275-350.

Linen - Italy, 48" round, fine linen with figural net lace inserts, cutwork, rose filet net lace edge, and embroidery, c. 1890-1970, $125-150; 60" round, $150-225; 72" round, $225-350; 84" round, $400-600; 96" round, $600-800.

Normandy Lace - France, 88" round, a mini patchwork of many Paris laces and embroidered fabric insertions, cream or white, all hand assembled, c. 1890-1960, $200-400.

Mixed Lace - France or Italy, 68" round, combination of drawnwork, embroidery, lace insertions, and Milanese-type lace border, all hand made, c. 1890-1940, $150-250.

Also available:

Cutwork - Portugal, 36" round, white or cream Irish linen with perfect cutwork and buttonhole stitches in flowing designs, c. 1900-1970, $50-75; 48" round, $75-125; 60" round, $125-175; 72" round, $175-225; 84" round, $225-275; 96" round, $275-350.

Damask - Ireland, 60" round, linen double damask floral or geometric pattern with a scalloped edge, c. 1880-1975, $75-100; 72" round, $100-125; 84" round, $125-150; 96" round, $150-200; 108" round, $200-250; 120" round, $250-400.

RUNNERS - Also called bureau scarves, these necessary items are to protect furniture surfaces. Most are rectangular or oblong as tables and dressers are those same shapes.

Appenzell-Like - Switzerland/China, 48"L x 17"W, when the demand for linens from the hamlet of Appenzell far exceeded the supply, common skilled needle workers from Switzerland and China were employed to copy the work as quickly as possible. Floral patterns were duplicated quite well while the figures were poor imitations of the original masterpieces, c. 1920-1950, $25-75.

Brussels Mixed Lace - Belgium, 46"L x 15"W, Point de Gaze raised flowers, scrollwork, and background braids are typical of Duchesse Bobbin Lace, c. 1850-1940, $75-100.

Chemical Lace - Germany/Switzerland, from 34"-66"L x 14"-18"W, fine but sturdy cotton
threads were made to imitate fancy old world needle lace, c. 1870-1955, $25-75.

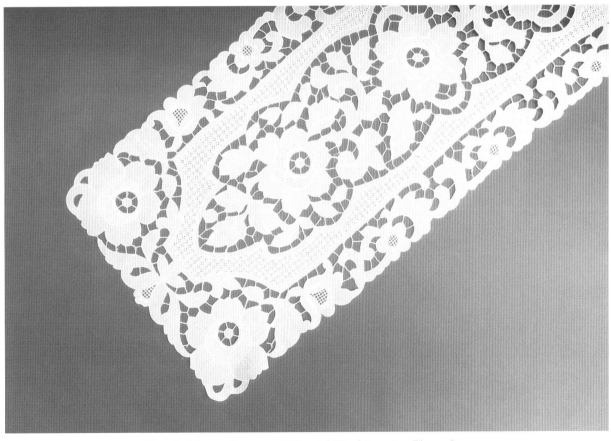

Chemical Lace - Germany, 48"L x 16"W, white cotton Plauen Lace
originally from a Five and Dime store with its paper label, c. 1940s, $18-38.

Colored Embroidery - America, from 34"-72"L x 14"-18"W, made from a prestamped kit, usually on heavy cream linen or cotton muslin, with added handmade or machine lace, c. 1890-1940, $15-45.

Embroidered - Portugal, from 24"-88"L x 14"-22"W, made on the island of Madeira of fine white Irish linen, usually with padded satin stitches in the basket, urn, or butterfly design, c. 1900-1970, $25-75.

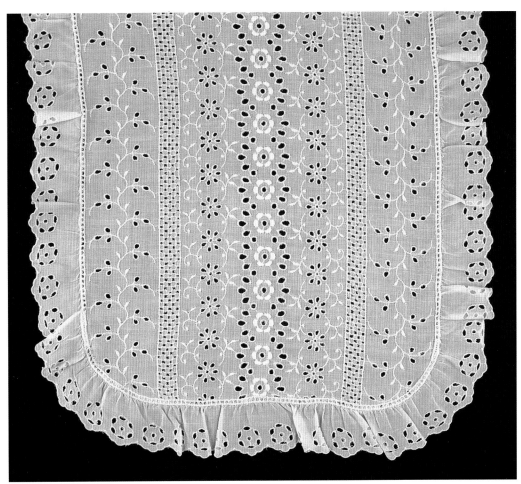

Eyelet - America, from 24"-54"L x 12"-18"W, cotton fabric with machine cut holes and stitched edges, often from the Five and Dime store, c. 1930-1970, $15-25.

France - 54"L x 17"W, fine linen with lavish needle-work, laces, and designs, c. 1890-1940, $75-125.

Handkerchief - England, 45"L x 13"W, three embroidered handkerchiefs crocheted together with lace edges that make one runner, c. 1920-1940, $20-30.

Limerick Lace - County Cork, Ireland, 38"L x 16"W, a fancy yet generic hand needle run lace of threads running in and out of the net background, c. 1880-1950, $30-60.

Needle Lace - Italy/Belgium, 52"L x 18"W, Belgium Zele or Italian figural cream cotton thread made with only a sewing needle and all hand assembled, c. 1900-1940, $65-95.

Needle run on Net - Germany/France, 34"-54"L x 14"-18"W, hand
needle run work on machine mesh net ground, c. 1910-1950, $25-55.

Princess Lace - Belgium, 34"-54"L x 14"-18"W, cream, hand
appliqués on machine net background, c. 1900-1950, $25-75.

Renaissance Lace - Italy, 42"L x 16"W, a generic tape lace design imitating early Milanese Bobbin Lace on fine linen with drawnwork, c. 1890-1940, $50-90.

Rice - China, 42"L x 16"W, rice linen (from the nettle plant) with embroidery and simple drawnwork, c. 1920-1960, $20-35

Tambour Work - Switzerland, 42"L x 16"W, fine cotton organdy
with machine backstitching tambour work, c. 1930-1960, $25-55.

Also available:

Battenberg - America, 52"L x 18"W, plain white cloth
with pre-made tapes fashioned into stylized floral and
geometric patterns, also called Modern and tape lace, c.
1890-1925, $25-50.

Embroidered - Portugal, from 24"-88"L x 14"-22"W,
cream Irish linen with gray, olive, taupe, or coffee colored
embroidery floss with cutwork, c. 1900-1970, $20-50.

SACHET - A fabric holder to keep non-oily potpourri in storage areas. Dried lavender blossoms, wormwood, and rosemary are bug deterrents suitable for fabric sachet bags.

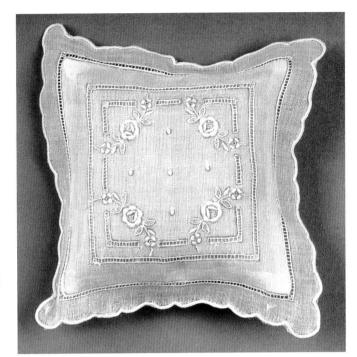

Holder - Switzerland, 4"-6" square, fine organdy with embroidery, drawnwork, and a button closure in the back for the sachet pillow, c. 1880-present, $10-15.

SHADE PULLS - Fabric shades were mounted to the frame of a window to block out sunlight, drafts, noise, and visibility. These hand crocheted pulls were strung from the center hole to pull the shade up and down without touching the actual shade, thus extending the life of the expensive shade.

Crochet - America, 1"-3", white or cream cotton crochet thread in lovely patterns, c. 1875-1975, each $5-7.

SHEET - An important household staple, usually dozens of sheets were found in early trousseaux. Bottom sheets began as flat sheets that were meant to cover the mattress ticking. Then, in the 1960s, the fitted bottom sheet became an instant success, hailed as a time saver for the tedious domestic ceremony of bed making. The top sheet was usually oversized to protect the coveted blanket from wear, tear, and soil. The most desirable and sought after linen top sheets have lavish cutwork, embroidery, lace, and monograms and are large enough to fit our modern queen and king size beds. Their fold over of 10" to 25" shows off the design and protects the blanket edge.

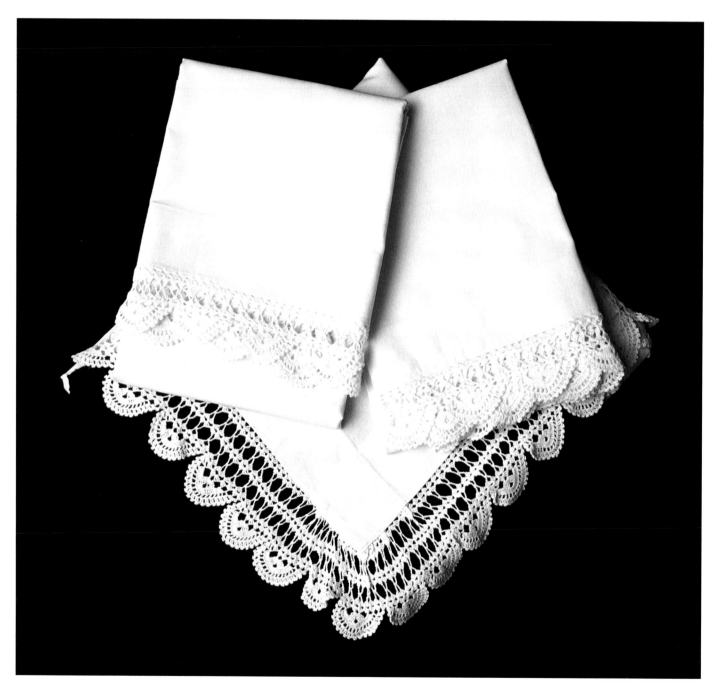

Crochet - America, 82"W x 100"L, white cotton sheeting with fine crochet lace on the top of the sheet and around both pillowcases, from a trousseau, c. 1930-1960, $100-125.

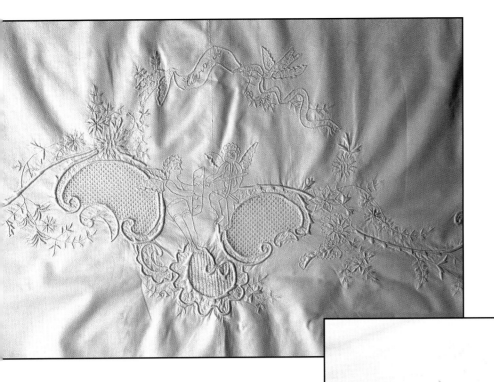

Above and right:
European - White or cream linen, linen/ cotton blend, or cotton with cutwork, embroidery, needle lace insertions, and lace edging, c. 1880-present, twin 72"W, $25-45; double 82"W, $65-85; queen 92"W, $100-125; king 106"W, $150-300.

Eyelet - America, oversized white cotton sheeting with machine made eyelet lace edging across the top and partially down the sides, c. 1880-1930, twin 76"W, $40-65; double 86"W, $75-100; queen 96"W, $100-125; king 106"W, $125-175.

Sheet 131

France - Unbleached flax yet silken enough for sleeping, this natural colored linen sheet and sham set has intricate drawnwork and needle lace mesh inserts of Point de France Lace with a monogram, c. 1880-1950, queen size 94"W x 114"L, $250-450.

France - 88"W x 108"L, snow white percale cotton with hand cutwork and hand embroidery with the bride's monogram of DR, c. 1932, $150-200.

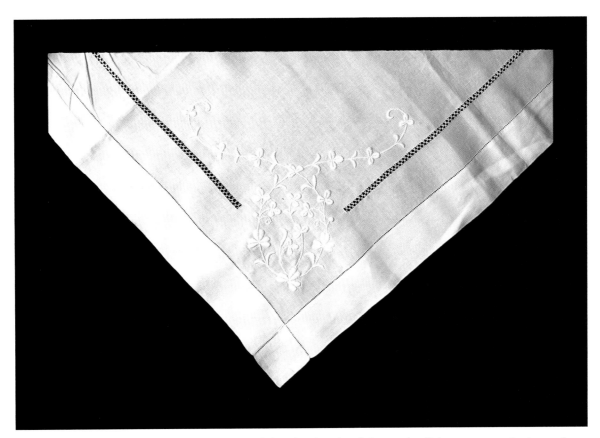

White Irish linen - Ireland, 88"W x 110"L, with hand embroidered shamrocks all the way across the top and hand drawn hem, c. 1900-1970, queen size, $125-200; with matching pair of pillowcases, $200-300.

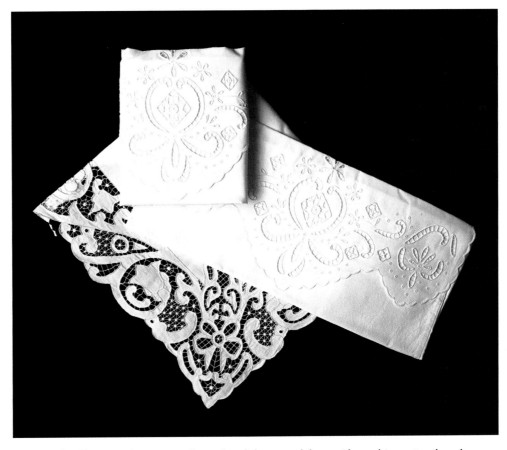

Italy - Fine percale cotton with a tailored drawnwork hem with machine cutwork and embroidery, c. 1920-1960, twin 70"W, $75-100; double 80"W, $100-150; queen 90"W, $150-200; king 102"W, $200-300; with matching pillowcases or layover shams, add $100.

Italy - Fine Irish linen with cutwork, embroidery, lace inserts, and a lace edge, c. 1900-1970, twin 72"W x 98"L, $100-150; double 82"W x 108"L, $150-200; queen 92"W x 112"L, $250-350; with matching linen pillowcases, add $100.

Italy - Machine cutwork and embroidery on muslin cotton with a paper label or stamped in washable ink "MADE IN ITALY," with unusual looking cherubs or scroll work, c. 1900-1975, twin 72"W x 98"L, $50-75; double 82"W x 108"L, $75-100; queen 92"W x 108"L, $100-150; with matching pillowcases or layover shams, add $50.

Italy - 92"W x 110"L, thick hand embroidery with the words "SONNO PLACIDO," double row of hand hemstitching, and added lace all on fine percale cotton from a wedding trousseau, c. 1900-1960, queen size, $125-175; with matching two or four pillowcases or shams, $200-300.

Madeira - Portugal, cotton percale with light blue, pastel, or white hand embroidery, cutwork, scalloped bottom edge, and a little lace with matching pillowcases, c. 1910-1975, twin 72"W x 98"L, $55-75; double 84"W x 108"L, $75-150; queen 94"W x 114"L, $150-250.

Also available:

Ireland - Impeccably rich pure white Irish linen with a tailored drawnwork hem, c. 1900-present, twin 72"W, $50-75; double 82"W, $75-125; queen 92"W, $150-200; king 102"W, $200-300.

Sheet 135

SHEET SHAMS - Just as pillow shams are to cover wrinkled pillowcases so sheet shams are also to cover the top edge of your wrinkled sheet during the day and are to be taken off at night.

Linen - Italy, 110"L x 36"W, the long, narrow piece was to cover your wrinkled sheet during the day and the pillow shams, 34"L x 34"W, were to lay over your wrinkled pillowcases during the day, all three were to be taken off at night, c. 1880-1940, queen size, $150-200.

Linen - Ireland, 104"L x 34"W, the long, narrow piece covered your sheet and the two cases, 32"L x 22"W, covered your pillowcases during the day and were to be taken off at night, c. 1880-1940, queen size, $175-225.

Eyelet - America, 82"L x 34"W, machine made embroidery and cutwork on cotton extending the whole length, c. 1930-1970, $50-75; with matching layover shams $75-125.

Linen - America, 110"L x 32"W, linen fabric with high quality handmade Battenberg lace, c. 1880-1940, queen size, $75-100.

Also available:

Cutwork - Italy, 98"L x 36"W, fine cotton embroidery with "SOGNI UNITI" (always together) hand embroidered in red or white floss in the very center with cutwork on all three sides, c. 1880-1950, $75-125; with matching layover shams $125-200.

Embroidery - Ireland, 92"L x 38"W, linen with sprays of flowers, shamrocks, and a scalloped edge, either handmade or machine stitched, c. 1890-1970, $100-150; with matching pillowcases or layover shams add $150.

Turkey Redwork - America, 88"L x 34"W, muslin cotton with bedtime sayings embroidered in red floss, the red dye for the floss comes from the bright yolks of turkey eggs, c. 1860-1915, $150; with matching layover or button back shams add $100.

SHELF TRIM - To add some color to an often dismal, dreary summer basement kitchen, fabric strips with colored embroidery were made to fit open shelving.

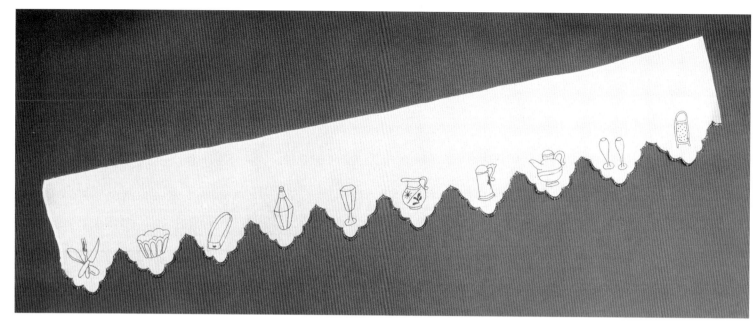

Embroidery - Eastern Europe, from 12"-200"L x 3"-6"W, hand embroidered kitchen utensils with any color floss, c. 1870-1950, $10-15 a foot.

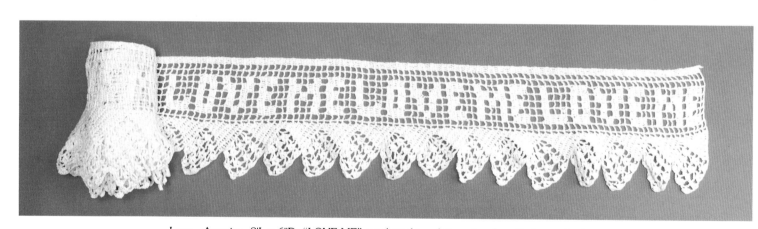

Lace - America, 8'L x 6"D, "LOVE ME" crocheted in white cotton lace that can also be used for towels, sheets, pillowcases, and tablecloths, c. 1900-1975, $15 a foot.

SPLASHER - A splasher's only purpose was to be attached to a wall or hung over the high bar of a washstand to prevent water from being splashed on the painted or papered wall as a person washed up from a pitcher and bowl set.

Linen - America, 24"W x 16"L, "SPLASH" embroidered in Turkey redwork on natural homespun flax with fringe on three sides, c. 1850-1910, $50-85.

Cotton - Eastern Europe, 38"L x 16"W, winged angel playing a flute in Turkey redwork on cotton with an added rod pocket at the top for wall hanging, c. 1870-1925, $50-85.

TABLE TOPPER - Originally, these table squares were made for card or game tables but since the popularity of these tables has passed they are now only used for decoration.

Alençon - France, 48"L x 48"W, machine made lace with a delicate cream mesh ground and a hand run needle lace design outlined with cordonnets, c. 1890-1985, $75-150.

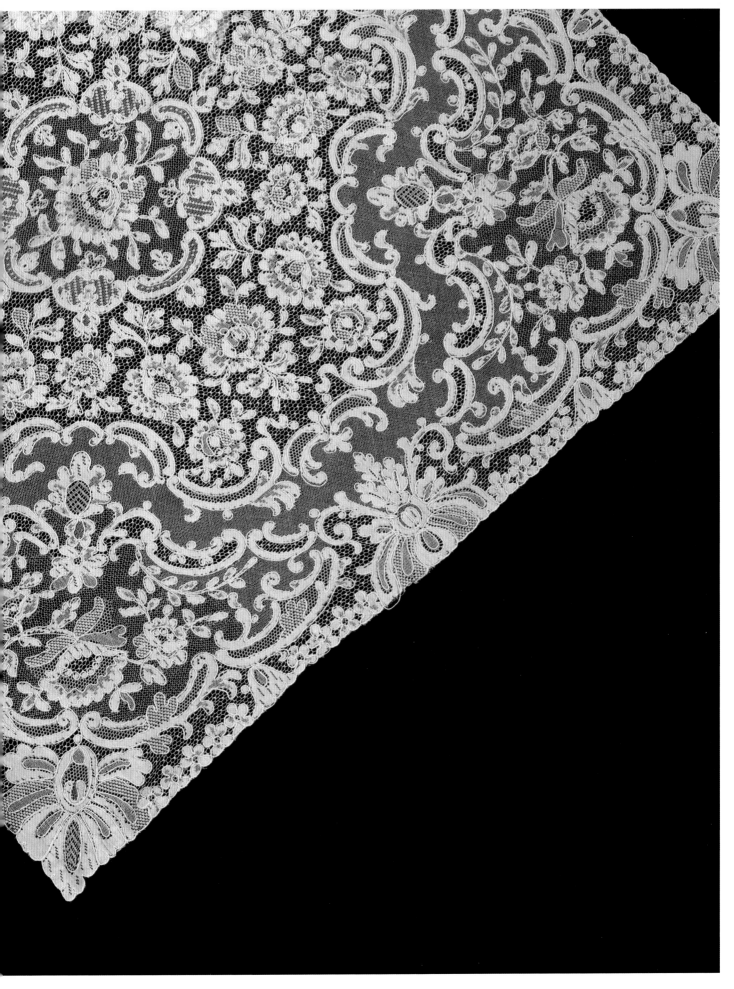

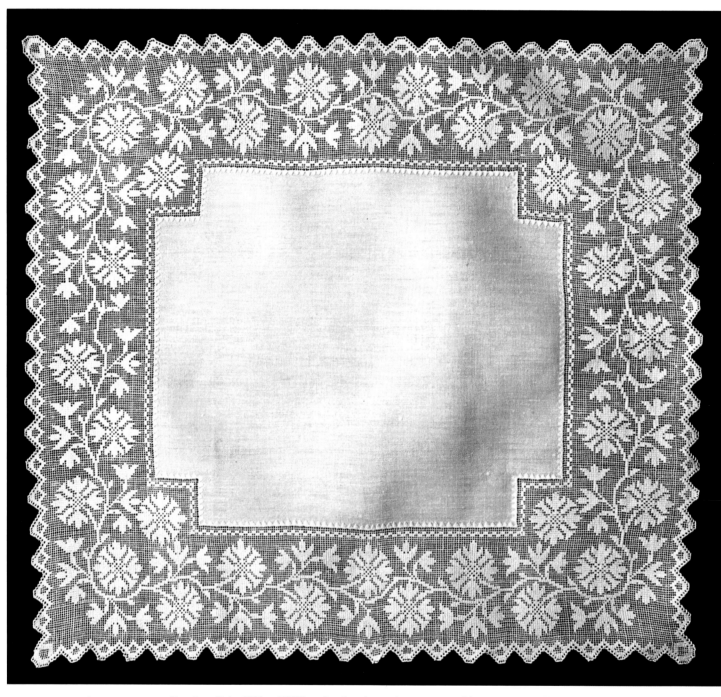

Buratto - Italy, 52"L x 52"W, stylized and angular grapes and leaves are needle
woven over a square grid called a leno weave, c. 1900-1950, $75-125.

Chemical Lace - Germany, 52"L x 52"W, fine white time honored cotton center with a chemically removed background imitating old world needle lace, cutwork, and embroidery, c. 1880-1950, $50-90.

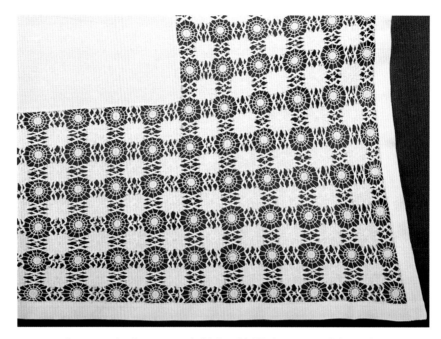

Drawnwork - International, 38"L x 38"W, this is one of the earliest forms of lacework having been made for centuries. Drawnwork has been made in almost every country in the world on linen, cotton, and silk. The quality can be crude peasant lace to high quality fashion lace with added embroidery, c. 1900-1965, linen, $50-85.

Embroidery - Portugal, 52"L x 52"W, fine Irish linen with padded satin stitches and cutwork in a very unusual four-armed shape made specifically for a small round top table, c. 1920-1950, $45-65.

Linen - England, 44"W x 44"L, wonderful Irish linen fabric with fancy
English filet crochet lace insert and around the edges, with hand
drawn hem, c. 1880-1960, $75-100. *Courtesy of Beth Knight.*

Organdy - Portugal, 48"W x 48"L, sheer cotton organdy with pastel
appliqués, embroidery, and four to six matching 11"W x 11"L
napkins, c. 1930-1970, set $100-150. *Courtesy of Anne O'Brien.*

TABLECLOTH - Used to cover fancy lacquered formal tables or simple scrubbed top worktables, these everyday necessities are both decorative and functional.

Alençon - France, 110"L x 72"W, cream colored machine stitched needle lace made on a delicate mesh ground, outlined with cordonnet cording, and linked with brides without picots, c. 1890-1985, $250-450; with twelve matching napkins add $125.

Army/Navy/Air Force - China, 106"L x 68"W, alternating patterns of net darning and embroidered linen, c. 1940s, $100-150; with twelve matching napkins add $75.

Damask - Czechoslovakia, all sizes, with patterned double damask woven linen with various bands of color with six to twelve matching napkins, c. 1930-1960, $75-100.

Damask - Scotland, 88"L x 68"W, red and blue woven linen double damask with flax fringe and a rare paper label surprisingly stating its origin, c. 1880-1930, $75-150.

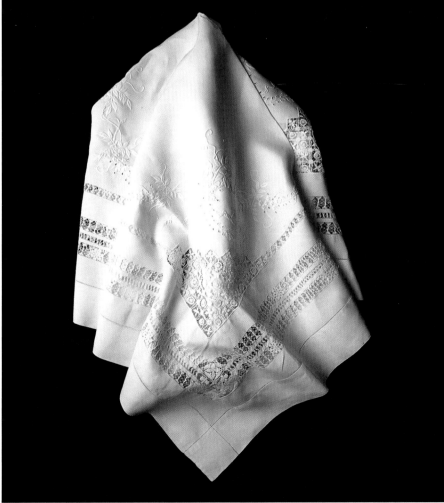

Drawnwork - Eastern Europe, 92"L x 66"W, white linen with wonderful hand drawnwork and added wisteria pattern hand embroidery, c. 1920-1960, $100-150.

Tablecloth 149

Kitchen - America, any size and shape, heavy duty cotton with wonderful
colored floral printed patterns, c. 1930-1960, $40-80; linen, $50-100.

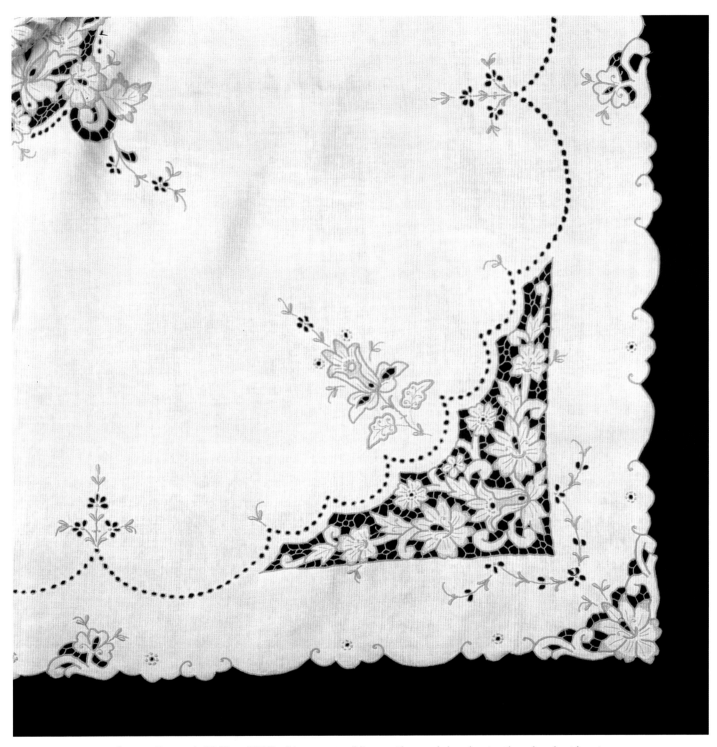

Linen - Portugal, 104"L x 68"W, white or natural linen with superb hand cutwork and embroidery in blue, white, taupe, or tan thread, c. 1900-1975, $100-200; 116"L x 68"W, $150-250; 128"L x 70"W, $200-300; 140"L x 72"W, $250-350; with twelve matching napkins, add $100.

Mosaic - Italy/France/Austria, 36"-60" square, white linen with a lovely floral punchwork pattern and often figures, c. 1915-1955, $50-100; 72"-96"L x 66"-72"W, $100-200; 98"-124"L x 66"-72"W, $200-400; with twelve matching napkins add $125.

Below:
Needle Lace - Italy, 36"-66" square, ecru linen with cream embroidery, flaxen needle lace inserts, and a lace edging, c. 1890-1950, $75-200; 102"-124"L x 66"-74"W, $250-450; 126"-144"L x 66"-74"W, $475-675; with matching napkins add $150.

Net Darning - Italy, 36"-68" square, ecru net background with hand needle run patterns, c. 1890-1950, $75-100; 102"-124"L x 66"-76"W, $100-200; 126"-144"L x 66"-76"W, $200-400.

Nottingham Lace - England, 110"L x 68"W, loom made lace imitating old world floral patterns with a heavy buttonhole stitched edge to prevent unraveling, c. 1880-1970, $50-100.

Organdy - Switzerland, 36"-68" square, pastel cotton organdy with white or pastel appliqués and tambour stitching, c. 1920-1970, $25-55; 72"-102"L x 66"-72"W, $75-150; 104"-124"L x 66"-72"W, $150-250; 126"-144"L x 66"-72"W, $250-350; with twelve matching napkins add $100.

Portugal - Madeira, 104"L x 66"W, fine white cotton organdy with pastel floral appliqués, linen fabric border, and eight matching napkins, c. 1930-1960, $200-300.

Quaker Lace - America, 88"L x 68"W, Nottingham machine made floral cotton lace imitating beautiful European lace, c. 1940-1990, $50-75; figural pattern, $75-125.

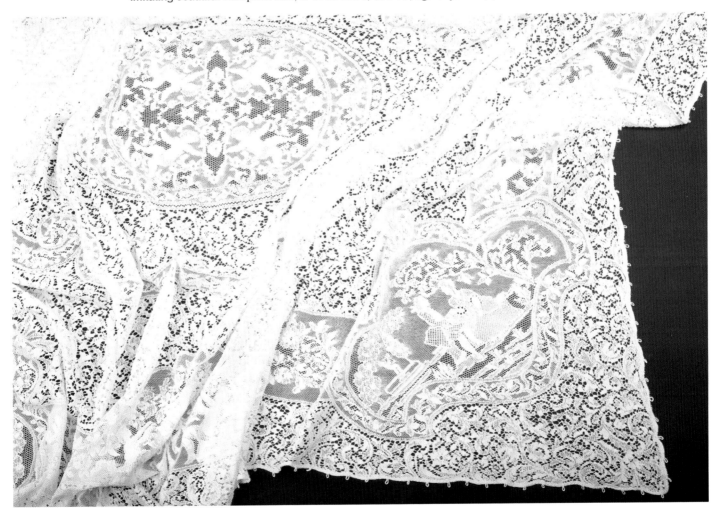

Tea Cloth Set - Madeira, Portugal, 34"L x 34"W, Marghab hand embroidery with appliqués on fine organdy with four matching napkins in the Iris pattern, c. 1934-1978, $150-250.

Also available:

Appenzell - Switzerland, 102"L x 68"W, fine white linen, intricate floral embroidery resembling a flurry of snowflakes and Buratto lattice work, c. 1900-1975, $500-800; with figures, $1,000-5,000.

Battenberg Lace - America, 68"L x 68"W, white cotton fabric decorated with pre-made tapes creatively arranged in floral and geometric patterns, ornamental spider web-type fillings, and rings covered with buttonhole stitches, c. 1880-1940, $125-200.

Crochet Lace - America/Eastern Europe, 88"L x 68"W, ecru or white cotton crochet thread in lovely swirling and pinwheel patterns that are flat to sufficiently stabilize stemware, c. 1930-1970, $75-100.

Cross Stitched - America/Eastern Europe, 92"L x 68"W, medium weight creamy linen with a pre-stamped pattern and six matching napkins, c. 1890-1945, $45-95.

Damask - United Kingdom, 68"-102"L x 68"-90"W, stately white double damask woven linen with any floral, geometric, or satin band pattern, c. 1880-1975, $1 an inch long; 104"-144"L x 68"-92"W, $1.25 an inch long; 146"-180"L x 72"-92"W, $1.50 an inch long; 182"-206"L x 72"-104"W, $2.00 an inch long; with twelve matching napkins add $125.

Damask - United Kingdom, 68"-102"L x 68"-90"W, well appointed white double damask woven linen with painted flowers, c. 1920-1975, $1.25 an inch long; 104"-144"L x 68"-92"W, $1.50 an inch long; with twelve matching napkins add $125.

Damask - United Kingdom, 68"-102"L x 68"-90"W, colored double damask woven linen with any floral, geometric, or satin band pattern, c. 1925-1975, $1.50 an inch long; 104"-144"L x 68"-92"W, $1.75 an inch long; with twelve matching napkins add $150.

Drawnwork - China, 84"L x 70"W, coarse white cotton with low quality drawnwork, c. 1920-1960, $50-75.

Embroidered - Eastern Europe, cross stitched colored embroidery floss on cream or white linen, 82"L x 66"W, c. 1920-1960, $45-75.

Kitchen - America, any size, heavy cotton with colorful patterns of the fifty states, c. 1930-1970, $50-100.

Luncheon - United Kingdom/Czechoslovakia, any size, cream or white linen with colored bands woven into the damask pattern with a hand drawn hem and matching napkins, c. 1925-1965, $50-150.

Net Darning - China, 36"-68" square, white or ecru net background with a heavy needle run loosely woven pattern, c. 1920-1970, $25-45; 70"-102"L x 68"W, $75-100.

Normandy Lace - France, 36"-66" square, hand assembled cream Paris Lace with embroidered fabric medallions, c. 1900-1950, $150-350; 80"-102"L x 66"-76"W, $350-450.

Organdy - Portugal, 36"-68" square, finely woven pastel, white, or cream cotton organdy with hand embroidery, appliqués, and some cutwork, c. 1925-1975, $25-55; 72"-102"L x 66"-72"W, $100-200; 104"-124"L x 66"-72"W, $200-300; 126"-144"L x 66"-72"W, $300-500, with twelve matching napkins add $125.

Punchwork (also called Mosaic) - Italy, 36"-68" square, medium weight cream linen with larger than average punchwork, c. 1915-1955, $25-55; 72"-98"L x 66"-72"W, $75-125; 100"-124"L x 66"-72"W, $125-200.

Rayon - Czechoslovakia/France/Ireland, 36"-66" square, white, cream, or pastel, lovely floral and figural patterns often with hand painted flowers, and matching napkins, c. 1930-1960, $25-55; 72"-98"L x 66"-72"W, $50-100.

Rayon - Japan, any size, any color, any pattern with matching napkins, low quality, c. 1930-1960, $15-75.

Rice Cloth - China, 36"-66" square, from the nettle plant family, rough white fabric with coarse embroidery, c. 1920-1970, $10-30; 78"-98"L x 68"-72"W, $50-100.

Tea Cloth - United Kingdom, 36"-48" square, fine white linen center with fascinating intricate deep filet embroidery edging, c. 1880-1975, $100-250; 48"-72" square, $250-450.

TABLECLOTH ENVELOPE - Made from a pre-stamped kit, these are to keep the tablecloth dust free and neatly folded. Companions are utensil and napkin wraps.

Wrap - America, 30"L x 30"W, cream linen with "TABLECLOTH" hand embroidered, c. 1900-1950, $15-25.

TEA COZY - A two-sided, half moon shaped cover with a feather, flannel, or cotton batting filled liner to keep the teapot hot.

Crochet - Scotland, 17"W x 20"H, fine white cotton filet crochet Tea Cozy with a Scottish thistle, c. 1880-1970, $45-75. Ivory linen with Italian needlelace inserts and ruffle, c. 1900-1970, $55-75.

Crochet - England, 15"W x 18"H, fine white filet crochet with "TEA" and a peach silk stuffed lining to keep the tea in the pot hot, c. 1880-1970, $55-75.

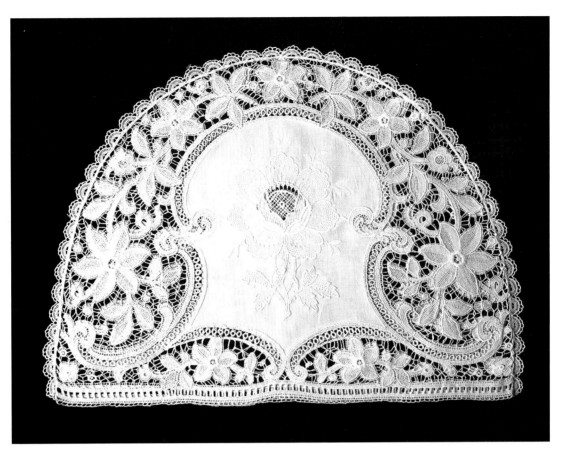

Lace - England, 15"W x 18"H, Schiffili machine made lace with an embroidered cotton center, c. 1930-1970, $55-75.

Linen - Madeira, 16"L x 14"H, apple green linen with hand embroidered dancing fairies, c. 1930-1970, $45-65.

Linen - United Kingdom, 14"L x 12"H, white cotton or linen with machine embroidery and a flannel liner, c. 1930-1970, $55-75. *Courtesy of Verna Scott.*

Silk - France, 16"L x 12"H, cream silk with hand embroidered violets, a monogram, and a feather liner, c. 1890-1945, $100-200. *Collection of the author.*

Also available:

Filet Crochet - United Kingdom, from 12"-16"L x 12"-16"H, white or ivory cotton crochet in a lovely filet pattern with a padded liner, c. 1860-1960, $25-125.

TOWELS - Used in either the kitchen, bathroom, or bedroom, towels come in many different sizes and shapes. Linen is the most desired fabric and huck the preferred weave. Linen fibers are lint free, hence their continued use as kitchen towels. Huck weave is a small nubby fabric that is highly absorbent. Fingertip towels are mainly found in guest bathrooms and bedrooms along with hand towels and body towels. Fine woven damask patterned towels often have monograms, fancy handwork, and lace trimmed edges. The fancier the towel, the more highly sought after they are today for home decorating and gift giving.

Appenzell - Switzerland, 22"L x 16"W, white Irish linen with extremely fine hand embroidery and Buratto work, c. 1900-1970, $75-95. *Gift from Carol Yahoub*.

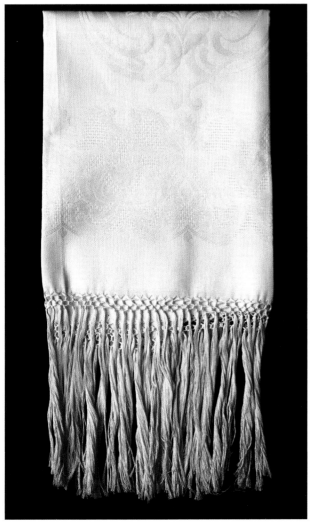

Bath - Italy, 48"L x 30"W, patterned damask linen, hand knotted flax fringe, often with a monogram, and/or a band of color with a paper label showing no use, c. 1900-1960, $50-90.

Bath - United Kingdom, 42"L x 26"W, patterned Irish linen, rows of hand
drawnwork, and a knotted flax fringe, c. 1900-1960, pair $100-125.

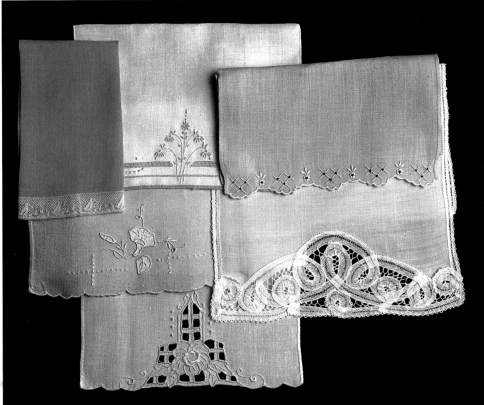

Above and left:
Fingertip - Eastern Europe, all about 12"L x 6"W, all are linen, some with appliqués, cutwork, embroidery, and organdy inserts, all hand stitched, to be placed in the powder room for visiting guests to use, c. 1890-1970, each $10-20.

Guest - America, 16"L x 10"W, hand embroidered "GUEST" on peach linen, c. 1930-1960, $15-20.

Guest - America, 24"L x 12"W, white huck linen with a strip of handmade insertion filet crochet lace saying "OUR GUEST," c. 1930-1960, $25-45.

Fingertip - Portugal, 10"L x 5"W, light blue linen with figural appliqués on organdy, c. 1925-1975, pair $25-45.

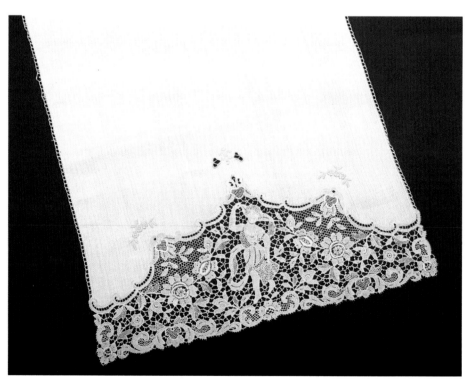

Guest - Germany, 21"L x 11"W, figural machine made Plauen Lace on cream linen, c. 1920-1950, $50-75.

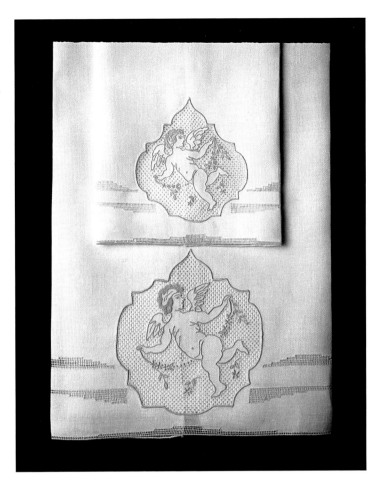

Guest - China, any size, Appenzell-type figural towels with a Buratto-type background and straight drawnwork on white linen with light blue embroidery, c. 1920-1960, set $100-200.

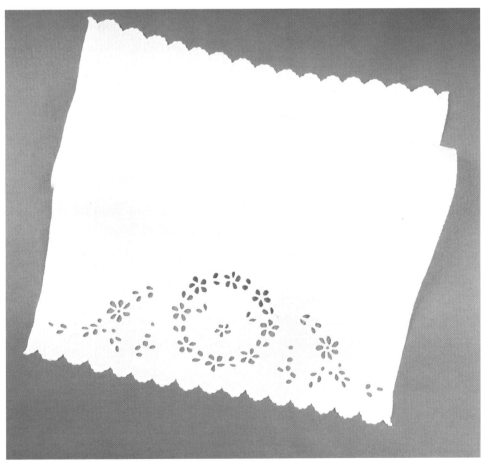

Hand - Portugal, any size, either huck or smooth linen with cutwork, embroidery, and/or lace, c. 1900-1970, $10-30.

Hand - Sweden, any size, huck linen with hand needle run colored embroidery floss on the top side only, c. 1900-1970, $20-40.

Right:
Hand - Madeira, any size, with pastel or white linen and organdy inserts of fish, c. 1930-1970, each $25-35.

Hand - America, any size, hand appliquéd floral design on white or cream linen, c. 1925-1945, $20-30.

His & Hers - America, 18"L x 12"W, a wedding present in 1943 with pastel linen and attached machine made lace, c. 1943, pair $35-55.

Kitchen - America, 24"L x 14"W, seven-days-a-week set neatly embroidered from a pre-stamped kit on linen, c. 1920-1950, set $75-100.

Kitchen - America, 180"L x 18"W, nubby linen
all purpose toweling with any color side bands,
c. 1900-1950, $75-125.

Kitchen - America, 28"L x 18"W, vibrant colored towels with Black
Americana theme, never used, c. 1940-1960, pair $100-150.

Kitchen – America, 26"L x 18"W, bold print of a Black Americana Mammy and child on medium weight cotton, used, c. 1940-1960, $55; pair $100-125.

Kitchen - America, 26"L x 16"W, bold colored prints of fruit, flowers, and vegetables on medium weight cotton, c. 1930-1960, $25-75.

Kitchen - Ireland, 30"L x 15"W, medium weight linen with colored cotton bands, c. 1890-1970, $15-35.

Kitchen - America, 26"L x 16"W, whimsical colored embroidery on
linen toweling, often with fringe, c. 1930-1960, $15-25.

Kitchen - Italy, 36"L x 18"W, "BUON GIORNO" hand embroidered in white cotton floss on white
damask with a grape and leaf pattern and hand knotted fringe, c. 1920-1960, $50-75.

Kitchen - Scotland, all about 38"L x 18"W, natural linen flax with bands of color, some with drawnwork, all on patterned damask linen, all have hand knotted fringe, all in unused condition, c. 1880-1940, each $25-55.

Lipstick - America, 9"L x 5"W, always on red fabric, these are to be placed
in the powder room for lipstick blotting, c. 1925-1965, set $15-25.

Lipstick - America, 10"L x 6"W, boxed hostess gift of red towels to be placed in the powder room for lipstick blotting, c. 1925-1965, set $25-50.

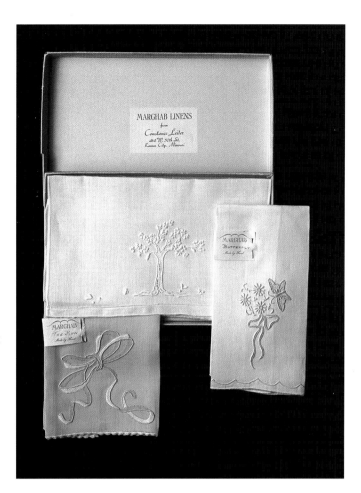

Marghab - Madeira, fingertip size, all about 14"L x 10"W, all on Irish linen in the Jacaranda Tree, Butterfly and Bow, and The Bow pattern, original tags and box increase the value of these towels, c. 1934-1978, each $50-75.

Above and right:
Monogrammed - Ireland, any size, patterned double damask or huck linen with a single hand embroidered padded satin stitched monogram, c. 1880-1970, each $25-75.

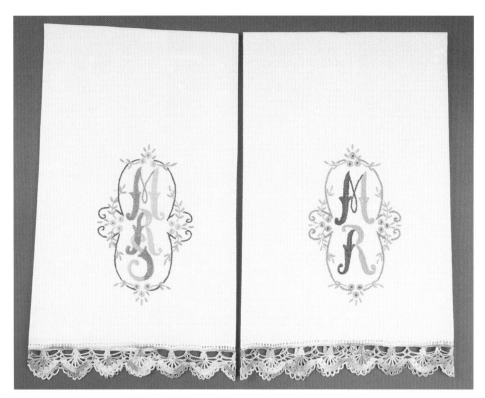

Mr. & Mrs. - America, 18"L x 12"W, a wedding present with
hand embroidery and crochet lace, c. 1947, pair $50-75.

Mr. & Mrs. - America, 22"L x 12"W, from the local dime store, these pure linen
towels were factory made yet have hand embroidery, c. 1940-1960, pair $20-40.

Risqué - Madeira, 18"L x 12"W, whimsical figures with padded body enhancements, all on linen with hand appliqué and drawnwork, c. 1930-1960, each $50-75.

Shaving - Czechoslovakia, 32"L x 18"W, patterned double damask linen with a band of colored rayon that is very tailored for a man's use, c. 1900-1960, $25-55; with a fringed edge, $50-80.

Shaving - Germany/Ireland, 28"L x 16"W, patterned double damask
linen with a tailored drawnwork hem, c. 1880-1970, pair $25-75.

Show - America, 22"L x 12"W, cream linen with added filet
crochet insert and a fringed edge, c. 1890-1940, $25-45.

Show - Italy, 49"L x 24"W, white huck linen with a padded embroidered B monogram, net lace insertion, Rose filet lace edge, and hand embroidery, to be placed on the door of the guest room to show off one's best needlework, c. 1880-1950, $50-75. *Courtesy of Linda Stevenson.*

Show - (Top) France, 52"L x 22"W, white huck linen with hand embroidered padded stitches and cutwork. (Middle) Portugal, 48"L x 23"W, white huck linen with cutwork and hand embroidered buttonhole stitches. (Bottom) Italy, 50"L x 26"W, white huck linen with hand embroidery, needle lace insertion, and rose filet edge. All c. 1880-1950, $50-75.

Tea - America, all about 22"L x 13"W, whimsical, fun linen towels used at teatime to be placed in the powder room for guests, c. 1930-1960, each $25-35.

Tea - Belgium, any size, linen with an edge of tape lace, c. 1920-1970, pair $25-55.

Tea - China, any size, cross stitched colored embroidery on cream linen, c. 1920-1970, $15-35.

Tea - America, any size, whimsical hand embroidery on linen toweling with a machine
lace border, usually available from the local dime store, c. 1930-1960, $15-20.

Tea - Madeira, any size, fine shadow work within an organdy insert
on linen, all hand stitched, c. 1930-1960, pair $55-75.

Tea - United Kingdom, any size, Irish linen with
insert of fine filet crochet, c. 1870-1970, $20-50.

Also available:

Finger Bowl - China, 10"L x 6"W, white linen with
blue thread hand embroidery, block style drawnwork, and
always in a set of six or twelve to be used at the dinner
table, c. 1910-1960, set of six, $30-60.

TRAY CLOTH - To be placed between a silver tea
service and the tray to prevent scratches.

Embroidery - Ireland, 22"L x 16"W, white Irish linen with machine
stitched green embroidery in the original box, c. 1950-1980, $10-25.

Lace - America, 20"L x 14"W, white filet crochet lace, c. 1965, *made by the author*, priceless.

Lace - Germany, 18"L x 13"W, white figural chemical Plauen Lace with a linen center, c. 1880-1950, $40-65.

Lace - Italy, 19"L x 15"W, cream cotton needle lace with a linen center, c. 1890-1960, $45-75.

Lace - United Kingdom, 18"L x 12"W, patterned white filet crochet lace, c. 1880-1980, $25-50.

Linen - England, 24"L x 16"W, white or cream linen with hand crocheted lace
inserts to fit a tea trolley or cart, c. 1880-1980, $45-75.

UTENSIL HOLDER - Purchased in kit form, these felt lined keepers prevent sterling flatware from tarnishing. Companion keepers are for napkins and tablecloths.

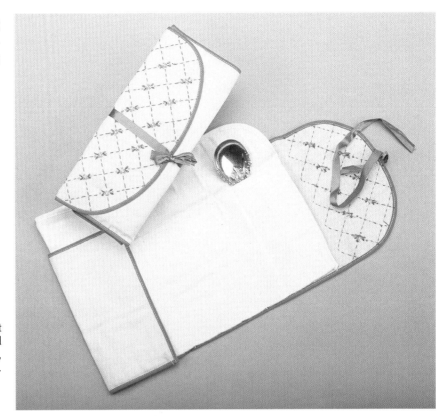

Linen - America, any size, felt lined cream linen with hand embroidery and silk ties, c. 1910-1940, pair $25-50.

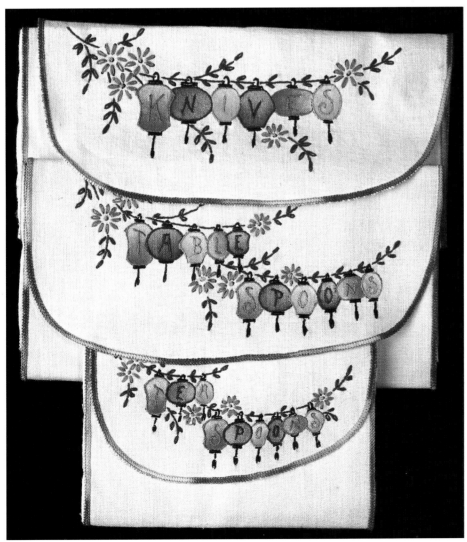

Linen - America, any size, any amount, felt lined linen keepers for tableware utensils that were purchased through a ladies magazine to be hand embroidered, c. 1910-1950, three piece set, $45-75. *Courtesy of Toby Barton.*

VANITY SET - Three piece coordinating sets that were
meant for deep-well dressers and ladies vanities.

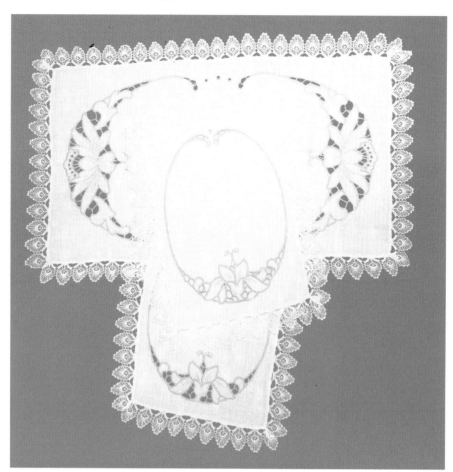

Cutwork - America,
any size, cream linen
with embroidery,
cutwork, and
machine lace trim,
c. 1930-1950,
$25-55.

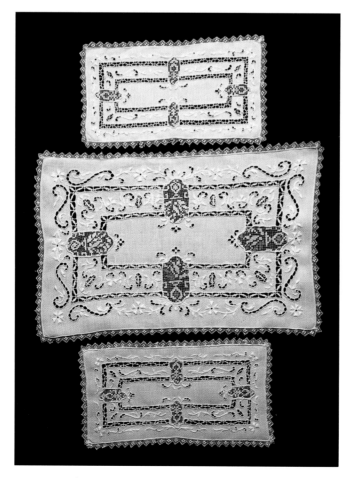

Cutwork - Italy, any size, crisp white linen
with padded satin stitches, net lace inserts,
and a lace edge, c. 1900-1950, $45-65.

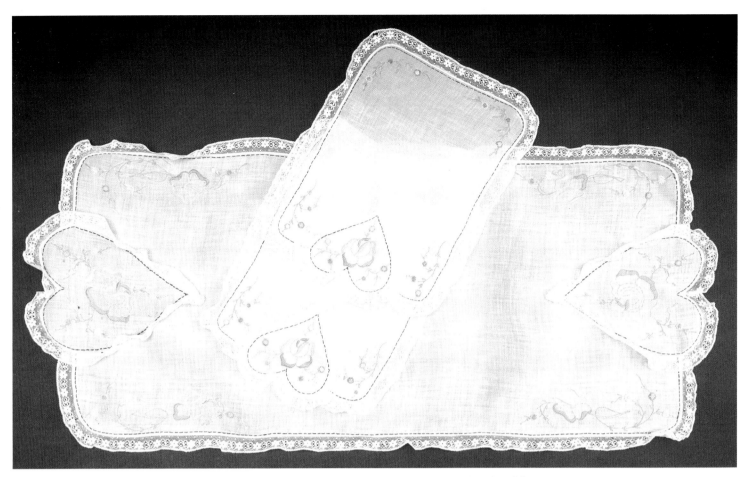

Embroidery - America, any size, white cotton with embroidered flowers
from a pre-stamped kit with machine made lace, c. 1915-1940, $25-55.

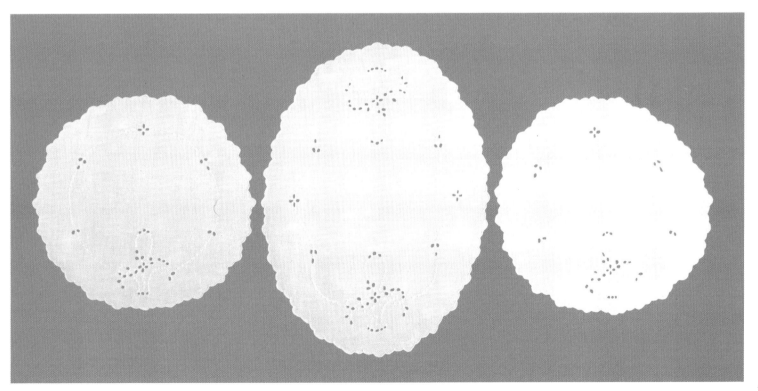

Linen - Portugal, any size, Irish linen with cutwork, padded satin
stitched embroidery, and often lace, c. 1920-1960, set $35-65

Bibliography

Bonito, Debra S. *Graced By Lace*. Atglen, Pennsylvania: Schiffer Publishing Ltd., 2001.

Cline, D.J. *Perfection, Never Less*. South Dakota: South Dakota Art Museum, 1998.

Gadsby, Chet. *Victorian Paisley Shawls*. Atglen, Pennsylvania: Schiffer Publishing, Ltd., 2002.

Hart, Cynthia and Catherine Calvert. *The Love Of Lace*. New York: Workman Publishing, 1992.

Homer, Aida Leake. *Official Price Guide, Linens, Lace, And Other Fabrics*. New York: House of Collectibles, 1991.

Kurella, Elizabeth M. *Guide To Lace And Linens*. Virginia: Antique Trader Books, 1998.